HOPE in the
WILDERNESS

Text copyright © David Winter 2003
The author asserts the moral right
to be identified as the author of this work

Published by
The Bible Reading Fellowship
First Floor, Elsfield Hall
15–17 Elsfield Way, Oxford OX2 8FG
ISBN 1 84101 258 0

First published 2003
10 9 8 7 6 5 4 3 2 1 0

Acknowledgments
All scripture quotations are taken from The New Revised Standard Version
of the Bible, Anglicized Edition, copyright © 1989, 1995 by the Division
of Christian Education of the National Council of the Churches of Christ
in the USA, and are used by permission. All rights reserved.

A catalogue record for this book is available from the British Library

Printed and bound in Great Britain by
Bookmarque, Croydon

HOPE in the
WILDERNESS

DAVID WINTER

BIBLE READINGS FROM ADVENT TO EPIPHANY

CONTENTS

INTRODUCTION

The world has many stories. Some make us laugh, some make us cry; some we forget and others we remember all our lives. But there are a few, very few, that mirror the human experience so vividly and completely that they have themselves become part of that experience. This book retells and reflects perhaps the greatest of them all, the Exodus—the story of a group of men and women with a charismatic but flawed leader, making their way from slavery in Egypt to a promised land 'flowing with milk and honey'.

Their way was beset with obstacles. Some were geographical, like the Red Sea which barred their path. Some were military, in the form of hostile tribes whose land they needed to cross. Some were self-inflicted, through their own internal doubts and divisions. Perhaps the greatest obstacle was the wilderness itself, the hot and barren land through which their journey had to be made.

Here are the ingredients of a story which is, in the true meaning of the word, archetypal. It is the model and mould of every narrative of human endurance; and within it, in the details and personalities, as it were, are all our stories—the baby born to greatness, the crushing horror of physical slavery and the possibly even more dehumanizing effect of emotional and spiritual bondage, the anger and disappointment and disloyalty that marred the courage and faith of a pilgrim people. And at the end, there lies across the dark waters of Jordan the land of promise. This is the story of a particular tribe of people long ago, but it is also your story and mine, the story of every life and every family under the sun.

That is why it has so often lit up moments of human history. This is the story which 200 years ago shaped the spiritual songs of the black slaves in the cotton plantations of America as they looked across Jordan to a brighter future of dignity and hope. A hundred years before that, it gave the Welsh preacher William Williams of

Pantycelyn the theme of his great hymn 'Guide me, O thou great Jehovah, pilgrim through this barren land', with its hope of a future free from poverty and despair 'safe on Jordan's side'. Over and over again its narrative has been invoked in people's struggles against slavery, oppression and despair, probably most recently in South Africa during the heroic journey towards the freedom of the black and coloured population.

The Exodus is also a story with profound meaning for many people at the personal level. I began this book while my wife was ill in hospital and completed it in the first year of a painful bereavement. For me it became the story of a slow and arduous journey through a barren and desolate landscape towards a place of distant promise.

But of course, most crucially, this story has defined the people of Israel, who find in it their foundations of faith. They are a ransomed, redeemed and liberated people, brought by the God of their fathers to the land of promise. Every spring, in the festival of Passover, that event is re-enacted and celebrated, not so much as a piece of history but as part of the experience of each Jewish person, in the past, indeed, but also in the now. 'You brought *us* out of bondage,' they say, as the ritual is shared around the family table in New York, London, Moscow or Tel Aviv—and they mean it. What happened to that struggling band of pilgrims over 3,000 years ago is every bit as much the story of the people now as it was the story of the people then. In one sense, it's impossible to put a date on it, because this story is almost uniquely timeless.

It was this story, no less, which was retold on the night on which Jesus was betrayed, as he and his disciples celebrated the selfsame Passover. And it is this story which gives a rich history to the Church's eucharist, as week by week and all across the globe, millions and millions of Christians proclaim its fulfilment in this food for another journey and this promise of an even greater hope.

Author's note

This book is designed for reading during the period from Advent to Epiphany, although, of course, that is simply one option for using it. It begins with a reading for Advent Sunday, and then could be read on each day from 1 December to 6 January.

'Advent' means 'coming', a time when Christians prepare to celebrate the first coming of Jesus and look forward to his return, which we call the 'second coming'. This book is about one of the great departures and arrivals of history, culminating in the 'coming' into the promised land of the people of Israel. As we follow their pilgrimage and see how it is, in many ways, reflected in the life of every Christian disciple, these parallels will, I hope, provide a very suitable Advent reflection.

To follow the story fully, it is important that the reader take time to read not only the 'key verse' set out at the beginning of each chapter, but also the whole biblical passage indicated. Advent books in this series in the past have usually printed the passage out in full, but that would have made this book uncomfortably large! In any case, the story is so vivid and compelling that it should not prove an onerous task to read it. Indeed, it might require more discipline not to read on into the next day's portion than to restrict oneself to the one suggested.

The approach I have taken is what is technically known as 'literary'. That's to say, I have not concerned myself with questions of authorship, editing ('redaction', as it is called) or historical influences on the text. This is the story as we have received it, part of the scriptures, and it has proved to be the 'word of God' to Jews and Christians down many ages. As we make it ours this Advent, may it also speak to us in our own situations, and in a very different world from the one in which this story was first acted out.

'I AM THE WAY'

JOHN 14:1–6

Jesus said to him, 'I am the way, and the truth, and the life. No one comes to the Father except through me' (v. 6).

This book is about the wilderness journeyings of the people of Israel over 3,000 years ago, but because the journey from captivity to the land of promise is the story of every life of faith, we shall constantly see in their experiences reflections of our own. When Jesus was about to leave his disciples, he used the language of leaving and travelling to describe what was to happen to him, and subsequently to them too. 'I am going,' he said, and 'where I am going, you cannot follow me now, but you will follow afterward' (John 13:36).

His journey to the Father, however, had a particular purpose: 'I go to prepare a place for you... so that where I am you may be also' (John 14:2–3). He was to be the one who went ahead to prepare the way, to ensure that when they came to the Father there would be a 'place'—a dwelling, a place to stay—especially for each of them.

By these words Jesus sets the life of faith in the language of journey. We travel from birth, through childhood and adolescence, on to adulthood, perhaps to marriage and family, and eventually to old age and death. But—and this is the heart of his message to them—the journeying doesn't stop then. Across the dark waters of death, like those of Jordan in the story we are to explore in these pages, lies a promised land, and when we arrive there we shall discover that the world's saviour has 'prepared a place for us'.

But before we arrive, there is the journey, and it is unlikely that anyone's path through life will be pain-free, much less 'roses, roses, all the way'. As it was for the Hebrews, slogging their way across the inhospitable desert, so for us. There will be times of spiritual desert, setbacks and failures, doubts and fears. Yet through it all, if we have the eyes of faith to see it, the 'pillar of cloud' by day and the 'pillar of fire' by night will go with us, as it did with them. Jesus would not leave his disciples 'orphaned', he said. He was going away, but only in order to be with them in a deeper and more lasting way.

The Advent themes are usually seen as death, judgment and the coming of Christ, and it's healthy that we should from time to time give thought to these sombre truths. But in one sense they are not so much sombre as realistic. The Israelites constantly came under the judgment of God. They lived in peril of their lives. They could only look forward, sometimes with fading faith, to the promise of a new land, rich in promise.

That was their story. It is also ours. We live under the justice and mercy of God, as they did. Our lives are mortal, however much we may trust in modern medicine to patch us up for a few more years. We can only look forward, like them, to the promise of a new life, where we shall 'know God and enjoy him for ever', as the Scottish Catechism puts it. Only? The story of the wilderness will tell us that it is not 'only', but all we need.

A reflection

As travellers on the journey of faith, we are strengthened by the presence of God, reassured by the company in which we travel, and clear about our destination. Like Jesus, we are 'going to the Father' (John 14:6)—and he is 'the Way'.

NOT WHAT WE WERE

EXODUS 1:1–11

Now a new king arose over Egypt, who did not know Joseph (v. 8).

It was hard to credit. This land, Egypt, was their home. At any rate, they knew no other, though the older people did talk of a distant land from which their ancestors came. Even the youngsters knew the names of those ancestors, the sons of Jacob: Reuben, Simeon, Levi, Judah, Issachar, Zebulun, Benjamin, Dan, Naphtali, Gad and Asher; and, of course, Joseph, the one they spoke of with awe, the foreigner who had become second only to Pharaoh and a power in the land. Because of him, the Pharaoh had ceded to his family the fertile land of Goshen, on the east side of the Nile delta and conveniently near to the royal palaces at Memphis. There they had settled, about 70 in all at that time. But that was long ago.

Now, in this warm and prosperous land, that 70 had multiplied many times over, until whole settlements of Jacob's descendants, the 'Hebrews' as the Egyptians called them, had sprung up in the land of Goshen. These settlements were not regarded favourably by the local people, who increasingly resented their presence. In fact, the new Pharaoh, who had come to power long after the era of Joseph, had recently been making speeches which were openly antagonistic. 'There are simply too many of them,' he argued. 'We can't risk a kind of fifth column in our midst, owing allegiance not to the ruler of Egypt but to some foreign power, and probably ready to support an enemy who chose to attack us. It's too big a risk—they've taken advantage of our openness and generosity. They see us, in fact, as a soft option.'

It wasn't just a matter of angry words. Ever since the first settlement by the sons of Jacob, the Hebrews had been indebted to their Egyptian hosts for the land that had been ceded to them. For many years that was no problem, because there was genuine gratitude for Joseph's wise leadership during the years of famine. But now, in a changed climate, land debt became an excuse for what was effectively slavery. Pharaoh proposed measures to restrict their numbers and influence in future, measures which turned the Israelites (literally, the sons of Israel/Jacob) into slaves, putting them to work on his new treasure houses at Pithon and Rameses and ordering the taskmasters to work them ruthlessly. The Hebrews reckoned that Pharaoh's intention was to make their lives so miserable that they would lose their enthusiasm for raising large families or, indeed, having children at all.

When the Hebrew elders met late at night in one of the little square brick houses of their settlements, these were the things they talked about. They had raised their complaints with Pharaoh himself, but had been brusquely rebuffed. Some of the elders could remember when their predecessors were honoured visitors at the palace, their opinions valued and their culture and religion respected —but not now. It was hard to take on board that they were no longer honoured descendants of the great Joseph, one-time saviour of Egypt in a time of dreadful famine, but despised aliens who had multiplied their numbers unacceptably and were to be treated as nothing more than free labour.

The outlook was bleak indeed. The Hebrews had lost respect and status and they were suffering daily actual physical persecution. Not only that, but there seemed to be little prospect of life ever getting back to the way it had been. They felt helpless, victims of circumstance, at the mercy of people who didn't like them, had total power over them and treated them contemptuously. Often, such times in life are the product or conseqeunce of our own ineptitude, failure or sin. For the Hebrews, however, they could see no reason for it. There was simply no justice in it at at all.

As the elders talked into the night, their ears full of the problems and pains of the people, their own bodies aching with the day's toil and some smarting still from the slave-masters' whips, they could not have guessed that the God of their fathers—by whom, if truth were told, they felt abandoned—was already secretly moving towards their blessing.

In a simple mud hut in the Hebrew settlement in Goshen, a pregnant young woman was wondering what would be the fate of her unborn child. Parents dream dreams for their children, but it must have been hard for her to think of a future for hers which would not be shaped by slavery, poverty and suffering. Yet in her womb, had she but known it, was her people's hope.

A reflection

It is always hard to find that we have lost a position we once held. Public respect, status and esteem are, quite naturally, things that most people value. It's a common side-effect of retirement or redundancy, for example, that one feels suddenly smaller and less significant. It can also happen as a result of widowhood or divorce—we are no longer as we were.

It's also not uncommon to feel that everything is going against us. What had seemed quite straightforward and promising suddenly takes a dive into the unknown. Life comes crashing in. At the best of times, such periods in life are frightening and bewildering, but they are doubly so when we feel helpless in the face of them, and especially when the very things and people in which we had put our trust suddenly turn against us.

It is in times like these that faith is tested, but it is also in times like these that we can discover in new ways what faith really means.

STANDING FOR THEIR PRINCIPLES

EXODUS 1:12–19

But the midwives feared God; they did not do as the king of Egypt commanded them (v. 17).

At dawn, as the people were setting off for another day's sweating toil in the harsh Egyptian sun, the Hebrew midwives, Shiphrah and Puah, sought out the elders. They were distraught, hardly able to speak. They had been given orders from Pharaoh that very morning that all male children born to Hebrew women should be killed at birth. How could they do it? It was against all they believed, a cruel distortion of their profession, which was to deliver babies safely. What were they to do?

There was no time for the elders to debate, but they said that they would talk with the midwives that night. Meanwhile, they should do what they could to keep the male children alive. Shiphrah and Puah took them at their word, and managed to deliver three male children that day, much to the anger of the Egyptian official who had been instructed to see that Pharaoh's instructions were carried out.

'We did our best to obey the ruling,' the midwives explained. 'But you must understand that the Hebrew women are of country stock, not like your soft Egyptian women. They start their contractions and go into childbirth before we can get there, as often as not. That's what happened with these three boys—they were already in their mothers' arms when we got to their houses. We were only told to see that the babies died during birth. We weren't told to kill them afterwards.'

Reluctantly, the official noted their explanation and sought clarification from the palace. By the time the elders met that night, the clarification had been forthcoming, but it wasn't good news. Rather than leaving things to the Hebrew midwives, whose commitment to carrying out Pharaoh's commands would always be doubtful, in future it would be the responsibility of the local Egyptian population to ensure that all Hebrew baby boys, newborn or not, were thrown into the Nile, to drown in its slow-moving waters. Given the current state of popular opinion about the Hebrews, who were blamed for everything from increased crime to food shortages, there would be little reluctance on the part of local people to co-operate fully with this command.

From the very next day, and with some enthusiasm, a search-and-destroy operation was conducted with ruthless efficiency as bands of men, and even some women, broke into Hebrew homes and snatched their baby boys—including some who were several weeks old—in order to throw them into the hungry waters of the Nile. The cries of stricken mothers rose from the streets of the settlements, terrible under the still night sky. The elders, talking long into the night, could see no answer. They were utterly at the mercy of the world's most powerful ruler in the world's most powerful nation.

Often in life, conscience collides with events. The midwives knew what they ought to do, which was to follow their consciences and the highest principles of their calling—which certainly did not involve collusion with the killing of innocent babies. But to follow their principles would certainly put them in peril of their lives, and probably would not in any case save the babies. Their answer was part subterfuge, part bare-faced cheek: they had an explanation for their failure to do what they had been told, and they were able to place the blame on what one might call a fact of nature. Hebrew women, of rugged desert stock, gave birth more quickly than the more urban Egyptian women. We don't know whether the Egyptian officials accepted their explanation or simply sought a less complicated and cruder answer to the problem. In any case, the result was the same—the babies were to die. But (and it is an important 'but') the midwives kept their consciences intact. And, just around the corner, as it were, millimetre by millimetre a foetus was being formed into a baby boy.

A reflection

In every walk of life there are moments when we are faced with this conflict between what we know to be right and what is expedient or comfortable. Much evil flows from the reluctance of those who should know better to 'get involved'. These situations arise in the home, at work, at school, in relationships and even in church. They may not be as dramatic or life-threatening as the one faced by the midwives, but they are real skirmishes in the great war between good and evil, and in that battle, ultimately there are no neutrals and no 'conscientious objectors'. The choice is ours!

THE POWERFUL AND
THE POWERLESS

EXODUS 1:20–22

So God dealt well with the midwives; and the people multiplied
and became very strong (v. 20).

The midwives had obeyed their consciences and the principles of
their calling, and God honoured that. But, as so often, principle was
in conflict with power, and the king responded with brutality. From
now on, *every* Hebrew baby boy would be killed, not by the midwives, but by the Egyptian people and their soldiers. This confronted
the Hebrew elders with a new problem, though their dilemma was
not an uncommon one. It had two demoralizing elements to it. The
first was their position as slaves, without status or respect. This
would have been galling at any time, but to have once enjoyed freedom and honour and now to have those gifts snatched from them,
as it seemed to them without reason, was devastating. The second
element was to be at the mercy of power so cruelly employed. There
was no court of appeal, no alternative jurisdiction open to them.
They could not leave the land (because their slave labour was now
too valuable to its people) and they couldn't do anything to change
their position.

Now it seemed that even their future existence as a tribe was
under threat. If no males were born, in the long run their numbers

18

would shrink, and in the relatively short term they would lose the element of youthful strength that any community requires. What could they do? What hope could the elders offer their people, beyond slavery stretching endlessly into the future, and mourning that would also be endless, as mother after mother saw her infant son snatched from her and hurled into the river?

As they talked, their thoughts kept turning to the past, not just to the quite recent past, when the previous generation had enjoyed the sophisticated pleasures of a prosperous and cultured land, but to the distant past. Someone mentioned Abraham, their forefather, a Chaldean who had left the great city of Ur to migrate westwards, taking with him his family, servants and flocks, driven by an inner voice that told him that this was what 'God' wanted him to do. But which God? There were many to choose from, but Abraham had begun to grasp a profound truth: there could be only one God, the ultimate source of truth and wisdom, and to obey his promptings was the principal duty of his creatures.

So Abraham lived in tents awaiting a word from God, until a series of divine visions revealed to him that he was to be the father of a great nation—one day, more numerous than the stars in the clear night sky above him or the grains of sand on the distant sea-shore. He believed the promise, and from that moment a new people was born, a people dedicated to the one true God.

The Hebrews, languishing under slavery hundreds of miles away in Egypt, were those very people, a people whose God was the God of Abraham, Isaac and Jacob. But where was he? It was all very well for God to call Abraham long ago; it was inspiring to think of his descendants, right down to Joseph. Their grandparents could remember many stories that their own parents had told them about Joseph in his days of power and splendour, and of his unshakeable faith in the God of his fathers. But where was that God now, in their moment of greatest need? It seemed to the elders, as it seemed to their people trying to settle to rest in their little houses on a hot, oppressive night, that it was the cruel gods of Egypt who held the real power. Was Abraham's God too weak to come to their aid, or perhaps unconcerned about their fate? With those disturbing thoughts, they made their way back to their families, able to offer them no promises of improvement, no hope of a better day tomorrow.

There is more than one kind of slavery, and many different ways to use power corruptly. In the ordinary traffic of life, we can become slaves by our own choice (to materialism, to a relationship, to success, drugs or alcohol or the equally deadly drug of envy and bitterness), or we can be enslaved by other people or circumstances. Most of us know what it feels like to be trapped, unable to free ourselves from something that we know is destructive.

There is also more than one kind of tyrant. Many people feel in thrall to a petty Pharaoh—the employer who demands 'bricks without straw', the relative who paralyses us into inaction, the child or sibling who seems able to dominate our decisions and rob us of our freedom. In the ordinary experience of life, such tyrannies can be as disabling as the one under which the Hebrews suffered 3,000 years ago in Egypt.

A reflection

Under any tyranny, we can easily fall into simple despair. No one hears our plea. No one cares about our situation. God himself remains silent and apparently aloof. We wait for promises and we look for a better day tomorrow. But as the Hebrews were to discover, we are often not only the victims of our circumstances but also part, at least, of the answer to them.

THE BIRTH OF MOSES

EXODUS 2:1–10

She named him Moses, 'because,' she said, 'I drew him out of the water' (v. 10).

Needless to say, many stratagems were devised by the Hebrew families to avoid the killing of their infant sons, but now that the Egyptians were directly involved, and the executions could be carried out long after the birth if it had been concealed, few of them were successful in the long term.

In course of time, the pregnant mother we have noted gave birth to a boy. She was of the tribe of Levi and the parents considered that they had a particularly fine little boy (though in truth all of the babies were regarded as 'fine' by their parents). For three months they were able to conceal his existence, but realized that when he started crawling and walking it would be impossible to keep up the deception.

The mother decided on drastic action. She made a basket, coated it with pitch so that it was watertight, and placed the boy in it. Under cover of darkness she took the basket down to the river and put it among the reeds at the water's edge. She knew that the royal princess, the daughter of Pharaoh, used that spot for bathing, and probably had a vague hope that something—who knew what?—might develop from that. Her older daughter was deputed to keep an eye on the basket and its precious cargo during the probable hours of bathing.

The plot, if that was what it could be called, worked to perfection. The princess and her entourage found the basket and the baby, who not surprisingly was crying. They recognized the child as Hebrew, but happily didn't call for the soldiers. Instead, moved perhaps by the child's tears and vulnerability, the princess decided to all intents and purposes to adopt him. At the right moment the sister emerged from hiding to ask if the princess would require the services of a wet-nurse to see the child through the weaning process. The offer was accepted, and she ran off to bring the boy's mother down to the riverside. The mother was charged to take the child home with her, nurture him until he was fully grown and then bring him to the palace. The princess would treat him as her own son—indeed, a member of the royal family.

The baby was named Moses 'because he had been taken out of the water'—it's a pun on the word 'water' in Hebrew. The name sounded sufficiently Egyptian to pass muster at court, and when the boy reached maturity he became known as Prince Moses. His nurse-mother had ensured that he knew all about his Hebrew parentage, culture and religion, but so far as his princess-mother was concerned, he was an Egyptian nobleman.

So the baby conceived in the simple home of a poor Hebrew family grew up with all the tensions of a mixed culture. He was a Hebrew by birth, and knew it. He was the child of a noble inheritance—a descendant of Abraham, no less—and understood and doubtless shared his ancestors' belief in a God who was above all gods, the almighty and eternal one. But by adoption he was a wealthy Egyptian, taught the dominant culture of that era, nurtured in the palace of the most powerful nation in the world.

That would have been his human *curriculum vitae*. In the divine scheme of things, of course, it was all rather different. His Hebrew provenance and his Egyptian upbringing would equip him splendidly for the most difficult and unlikely of all tasks. Fate, or the hand of God, was about to propel him into a role he certainly would never have sought and probably in his wildest dreams could not have imagined.

A reflection

It is not only with the great and gifted that God works his purposes. Time and again, if we have eyes to see it, he shapes lives to meet needs and fulfil his will. Reading the story, it might seem that Moses' parents, his sister, the royal princess and even Moses himself were simply pawns in some greater but as-yet-unrevealed purpose. But, in truth, at each stage, as individual human beings with a God-given will, they could have decided to act differently. Each of them, at each moment of decision, did what seemed the right thing to do, and God was able to take those choices and mould them into something infinitely greater.

INDISCRETION, OR COURAGE?

EXODUS 2:11–15a

He answered, 'Who made you a ruler and judge over us?' (v. 14).

Moses grew into a strapping young man, destined for a suitable marriage and eventually a position of power in the land, like his ancestor Joseph. However, one moment of indiscretion, or possibly moral courage, was not only to cost him his place at court but also to imperil his life.

It's never easy to live within two conflicting cultures, which must have been the experience of the young Moses at the Egyptian court. On the one hand, he had the history and religion of his Hebrew mother, who had told him of Abraham and the covenant of God—the one, true, living God, who had made great promises to the patriarch and his descendants. Yet, in the palace, he was living in the environment of the most powerful and pervasive culture of the ancient world. The royal palace at Memphis stood on the eastern side of the Nile, the side of the rising sun, of life and activity and fertility. But across the river, beyond its western banks, was the dark and sombre land of the setting sun, the place of the dead, where only vast tombs broke the barren contours of the empty desert. In his ears would echo the insistent words of his mother: 'There is only one God, the God of Abraham, Isaac and Jacob'. But his eyes could not avoid the gods of Egypt all around him, symbols of mighty power but also of life and death; and he knew that one day, if his life continued on its present course, they would be his gods, too.

Like many young people in his position, Moses hankered to know more of his own background and origins. Perhaps it was that which drove him out of the palace one day towards the great building-sites of the treasure houses at Rameses, where his own people, the Hebrews, were slaving under the fierce midday sun. As he walked around and saw what was going on, it would have been impossible for a person in his position not to have felt appalled. Perhaps one of these men stumbling under the lash of a slave-driver was his own father. Perhaps that little group, backs breaking under the weight of the massive stone they were manhandling, came from his clan, were his kith and kin.

Moses moved away from the main site, towards a place where a smaller group was labouring under the eye of a particularly brutal supervisor. When the man picked on one elderly victim, beating him repeatedly with his whip until the man was covered in blood and fell to the ground, it was more than Moses could tolerate. Looking around to check that no one was watching, he stepped towards them to intervene. He grabbed the Egyptian by the shoulder to pull him away from his victim. The slave-driver resisted, but the young prince was stronger and fitter, and with his bare hands killed him. Realizing the enormity of what he had done, and standing alone with the body on the sandy ground, he set about burying the man. The Hebrew slave had made his escape as soon as the prince had intervened, so Moses hoped that his involvement in the killing would remain a secret.

He returned to the palace, but was drawn, as if by a magnet, back to the same area the next day. Again he observed the sufferings of his own people. Again he was appalled by the cruelty of the slave-drivers. But this time what caught his eye was a sudden fight between two Hebrew men—exactly what one would expect when people are put under that kind of pressure under a hot sun. Moses could not resist intervening. 'Why on earth are you fighting among yourselves?' he asked. 'Isn't your situation bad enough at the hands of the Egyptians?'

If he had expected thanks for his peace-making efforts, he was wrong. One of the men turned on him, possibly not realizing that Moses was himself a Hebrew. 'Who made you our ruler and judge?' he asked. 'Were you thinking of killing us in the same way you did that Egyptian?' Moses had no answer, but as he made his way back to the palace he realized that the killing of the slave-driver was by no means a secret and, in the ordinary course of things, would eventually reach the ears of Pharaoh. When that happened, the consequences for Moses would be dire indeed.

That very night he decided on flight, leaving—for ever, as it turned out—the life of the royal palace at Memphis and making his way to Midian, in the desert to the east. He had no plan, indeed no idea what might happen to him. He just felt that he was safer there than in Egypt, and perhaps the silent desert would provide an opportunity to rethink his life... if he could survive its rigours.

A reflection

God was calling Moses. With hindsight we can see the process, but at the time, as events unfolded, it must have seemed to the young prince that all he was experiencing was a sequence of personal disasters. Certainly there is no suggestion that he, or anyone else, saw the hand of God at work in what was happening to him.

It is often hard to believe in the purposes of God, especially when from our own perspective things simply seem to be falling apart. Yet all of this—the bulrushes, the palace, the fight with the taskmaster, the flight to the desert—was the raw material of the call of Moses. Each of these experiences, refined and worked at by the Spirit of God, would make him the person God could use.

AN ALIEN IN
A FOREIGN LAND

EXODUS 2:15b–22

'Why did you leave the man? Invite him to break bread' (v. 20).

It was a relief to find an oasis with a well. After slaking his thirst, Moses sat by the well and watched as some young Midianite women, seven of them, brought their flock to water. As they were filling the troughs for their animals, a group of shepherds came along and tried to drive them away. Moses—who seems to have been the sort of person who simply couldn't avoid getting himself involved in things—came to their rescue, persuading the shepherds to leave them alone and then drawing water for them and watering their flock.

The young women, perhaps overawed at this gesture by an Egyptian nobleman and a stranger, neglected to offer him the customary hospitality. However, when they reported events to their father, Jethro, a Midianite priest, he told them to hurry back and invite the stranger to their home. Moses agreed to come with them, probably glad of the prospect of a meal and some shelter from the sun. In the event, he got rather more than that, staying at the family home as a guest and eventually accepting an offer from Jethro of one of his daughters, Zipporah, as a wife.

So began a strange period in Moses' life, covering several years. As with so many of those whom God has called to do great things, it seemed that he first must spend a period detached from the conflict, as it were: we can think of the time Paul spent in the wilderness of Arabia before his calling as an apostle (Galatians 1:17), or John the Baptist, 'who was in the wilderness until he appeared publicly to Israel' (Luke 1:80). Indeed, even in the experience of Jesus we have what some people have called the 'hidden years', from his teens to the age of 30, when he may well have spent time himself with John in the Jordan area, waiting for the moment of his commissioning at the Baptist's hands. These times may seem irksome—we want to 'get on with it'—but the timing is always God's, not ours.

Eventually Moses' wife bore him a son, whom he named Gershom (*ger* is Hebrew for 'alien') 'because I have been an alien… in a foreign land' (v. 22). Of course, by marrying a Gentile and starting a family, Moses would seem to have taken a major step away from his inheritance as a 'son of Abraham'. After all, by tradition the Jewish line is matriarchal, passed down through the mother to her sons and daughters, which would mean that Gershom was not a Jew. Moses himself, by 'marrying out', had signalled the fact that his departure from Egypt was not regarded by him as a temporary thing. Clearly he could not see at that moment how he would ever go back there.

It's interesting to speculate where exactly he would have located his homeland at this point—Egypt, the land of captivity, or the ancient tribal fields far away to the north, from which his ancestors had come? Or possibly Midian, this rock-strewn, barren land where he had been welcomed and now had a family of his own? At any rate, to all intents and purposes Moses had 'settled down', if so restless a spirit could ever be said to 'settle' anywhere.

A reflection

Observed from the 'inside', our lives usually look like a series of unplanned events—things that happened to us or around us, over which we felt we had little control. For instance, we are born in a place and to parents not of our choosing. We 'happen' to meet people who come to play a vital role in our lives—perhaps a marriage partner, a lifelong friend or someone who is a vital catalyst in an important process of change for us.

However, when we look back at life from some later vantage point, we often detect some kind of pattern or shape to it all. Christians would usually ascribe that to God's intervention or purpose in their lives. Certainly the life of Moses at this point must have seemed to him like a sequence of unplanned events, yet as the story unfolds it becomes clear that in the purpose of God they were nothing of the kind. As the apostle Paul wrote, 'In all things God works for good for those who love him' (Romans 8:28).

THE GOD WHO HEARS
AND RESPONDS

EXODUS 2:23–25

God heard their groaning, and God remembered his covenant
(v. 24).

Meanwhile, in Egypt, the Pharaoh of Moses' childhood had died, but
this, instead of bringing any relief for the suffering Hebrews, made
matters worse. At last something of the faith of Abraham seemed to
awaken among them, and instead of groaning and complaining
(natural enough, of course, but totally ineffective faced with a cruel
oppressor) they took to prayer, crying out to the God of their fathers
to rescue them from slavery.

The Bible gives us God's response. 'God heard their groaning, and
remembered his covenant with Abraham, Isaac and Jacob. God
looked upon the Israelites, and God took notice of them' (vv. 24–25).
God heard, remembered, looked and took notice. It might not have
seemed very much—after all, it was action that the Hebrews needed,
and quickly—but as things turned out, it was enough.

When we are under pressure of any kind, it is often easier to
complain than to pray. What the slaves in Egypt finally remembered
was that they were still the children of the covenant, even in slavery. It's interesting that in God's thinking the 'Hebrews' become
the 'Israelites'—the descendants of Jacob and the heirs of God's

promises to him. They might have forgotten God (an almost excusable fault in view of the kind of lives they were leading), but he had not forgotten them

It was only after 'a long time' that the Israelites, despairing of any human relief for their plight when the new ruler proved as intransigent as the previous one, finally 'cried out' to God for help. It's not hard to identify with them, for only too often our prayers, too, are real and urgent only when we despair of finding any solution to our problems ourselves. There is something desperately moving about the cry of the stricken heart, and it seems to fly straight to the heart of God.

Divine aid was now imminent. The God who heard, remembered, looked and took notice was the God who had never abandoned them but had been waiting for them to turn again to him. Not only that, but his plans were already on the move: long before their anguished prayers were heard, he had begun to answer their cries. A woman had conceived. A baby had been born and marvellously kept from slaughter. A young man had been adopted by a royal princess. And now Moses was in Midian... but to the young husband and father it probably came as a surprise to discover that God was there, too.

A reflection

It is a facet of Moses' character that he sometimes seems to act first and then try to deal with the consequences. It led him into many problems, but it also meant that he was a person of action rather than reaction. Was that why God chose him, perhaps? At any rate, it is a reminder that God works with our weaknesses as well as our strengths.

It is very typical of our human response to God that we turn to him only when all human channels of aid have failed. Yet he hears and works in mercy. Are there problems that I have been struggling to cope with in my own strength, instead of simply 'crying to God'?

THE BURNING BUSH

EXODUS 3:1–15

'The cry of the Israelites has now come to me; I have also seen how the Egyptians oppress them. So come, I will send you to Pharaoh to bring my people, the Israelites, out of Egypt' (vv. 9–10).

It took the young prince a while to adjust to the life of a rural sheep farmer, but he had little choice. He couldn't go back to the court at Memphis—or to his birth family, for that matter. He had married and been welcomed into the family of Jethro, who combined sheep-rearing with the role of a Midianite priest. Moses tried to keep in mind the beliefs that his mother had taught him, beliefs in the God of Abraham, Isaac and Jacob, his forefathers, but at times all of that seemed a fading memory.

He was an adventurous shepherd, needless to say, and on one occasion led his flock beyond the desert region into the foothills of Mount Sinai. Among the rocks ahead of him, something caught his eye. A bush, probably a gorse, was on fire. In the hot sun that was not very remarkable, but he was struck by the fact, as he made his way closer to it, that it seemed to be burning steadily rather than slowly consuming itself, as he would have expected. For a moment he stood there, quite transfixed by the sight of the flaming bush, and it was at that moment that he heard the voice of God.

Later, Moses may have asked himself how he knew that that was what it was, but it was not a question he could answer. It was simply an unshakeable conviction that what he could hear, whether in the private ear of his mind or the physical ears of his body, was nothing less than divine. He was told to remove his sandals as a mark of respect and then move closer to the bush. This, he was assured, was holy ground. Not only that, but the voice had the ring of truth about it: 'I am the God of your father, the God of Abraham, the God of Isaac, and the God of Jacob' (v. 6). Moses hid his face in his hands and waited for more.

It followed quickly and insistently. The voice told him that the cry of his people in Egypt had been heard, that desperate cry of the oppressed. Now the moment had come for their God to intervene on their behalf, to bring them out of slavery and lead them to a new home, a good land of milk and sweetness, far away in the land of the Canaanites. But to do this, God needed a human agent, and Moses was where he was at that moment in order to be that agent. He would go to Pharaoh with the express purpose of bringing the Hebrews out of Egypt—and when he had succeeded, they would all worship God on this very mountain. That promise was made in response to Moses' faltering observation, 'Who am I that I should go to Pharaoh, and bring the Israelites out of Egypt?' (v. 11). But it was prefaced by an even more significant promise: 'I will be with you' (v. 12).

Up till now, Moses had stood there motionless, head in hands, rendered incapable of movement or action for awe of the moment, but at this last revelation he was stirred to react. He must know for sure the identity of this voice. If he were to risk everything on what looked like a suicidal enterprise, he wanted to know who it was who was sending him on it—and rather more specifically than simply 'the God of his ancestors'. 'What is your name?' he asked.

The voice resumed with words that Moses would never forget: 'I am who I am.' That is my identity: I am. Tell Pharaoh that 'I am' has sent you, and tell the Hebrews the same thing—the God of their fathers has a name, which is holy and sacred. He is a God without beginning or ending, an eternal present tense. I AM. This is my name and title for ever.

Moses couldn't have known it then, but that was a defining

moment in the history of the human search for God. The one and only God, 'the God of his fathers', was not a tribal deity but a transcendent, eternal being, without beginning or ending. He was YAHWEH—'Jehovah', as the Hebrew letters have been traditionally (and probably wrongly) interpreted, 'the LORD', as the English translations render the sacred name. It was none other than the creator of the universe, himself beyond time and mortality, who was intervening in the history of this planet and the story of this one people, and it was his voice that spoke to Moses 'from the burning bush'.

The incident of Moses at the burning bush is one of the great turning points not only of this story but of the whole history of religion. Here is the supreme picture of the intervening God, one who heard the cries of those who prayed and then acted on their behalf. In recent times this has not been an entirely fashionable way of thinking of God. Modern people are perhaps happier with the idea of a God who suffers and identifies with his people without actually intervening in their lives. Yet in this story the first concept leads naturally into the second: God was suffering with the Israelites, he did identify with them, and it was because of that that he was now moved to action.

A reflection

God's action here, as it usually does, involved a human agent. Moses, the refugee in a foreign land, far away from the day-to-day plight of the people, was called to be that agent. Like everyone whom God calls, he had the awesome (and ultimately God-given) right to refuse. This is the deep challenge of vocation—that God calls us, but we have to say 'yes' or 'no' to his call. Sometimes we may not be clear about what he is calling us to do in a given situation. But as often—or even more often—the problem is not what we are called to do, but our willingness to do it.

OBJECTIONS OVERRULED

EXODUS 3:16—4:17

'I know, however, that the king of Egypt will not let you go unless compelled by a mighty hand' (v. 19).

Before Moses could fully grasp this revelation, the voice was telling him more, and even more urgently. 'Go back to Egypt. Gather the elders together and tell them what has happened today, and the message and promise that I have given you. Go with them to Pharaoh, and tell him on my authority to let you go and offer sacrifices in the desert. He will not let you go unless compelled to do so, but I will show my power and strike Egypt with such wonders that in the end he will let you go, and go for good, laden with spoil.'

Again Moses stood transfixed. Could this really be happening? Was he suffering some grand illusion, brought on perhaps by the heat of the day? He decided to question the voice. 'Supposing the elders simply don't believe me when I say that you have given me these instructions?'

'They will', said the voice, 'when you perform such acts as I shall make possible, transforming that staff in your hand into a snake, perhaps, or your hand itself to leprous white and then to health again. Can you not trust me?'

Moses tried another objection. 'I am no public orator. Indeed, I have been described as clumsy in my speech.'

'I do not need human eloquence,' said the voice. 'I shall be your mouth. I shall give you words.'

Moses tried one final request. 'I plead with you, send someone else.'

At this, the voice assumed an angry tone. 'See, your brother Aaron is already on his way to Midian to meet you. He is eloquent enough for both of you. You can be the voice of God to him, and he can be the voice of Moses to the people.' There was a pause, and then one simple command. 'Come now, take up your staff, and go.'

Among the many mysteries in this incident of the burning bush, the one that probably stands out most to the modern reader is the mystery of God's 'providence'. It is not hard to understand that God knew of the plight of his people in Egypt, or that he was moved by their suffering. More difficult for us, perhaps, is the notion that even before the people cried out for help, God was organizing events and people to make their eventual rescue possible. The baby Moses was saved from drowning and taken, through a remarkable sequence of unpredictable events, to the land of Midian, there to await a call from God which was totally unexpected. Now we learn that even before that call had been brought to him, his reluctance to respond to it had been foreseen and allowed for. His brother Aaron—hitherto a hidden figure—was already on his way to the desert in search of him and he would be Moses' colleague, companion and spokesman for the task that lay ahead.

It is futile to speculate how Aaron came to exist. Perhaps he was an elder brother, born before the Egyptians began to slaughter Hebrew babies. Or was he, too, hidden from the Egyptians by subterfuge? Or was he a much younger brother, born at a time when Pharaoh had abandoned the cruel and apparently ineffective strategy of mass infanticide? We do not know and we are not told, but Aaron had presumably grown up in Goshen and was now on his way to Midian in search of his long-lost brother. Whether his journey had been prompted by a vision, or was simply the consequence of family or personal concern, we are also not told. For Moses it was probably enough, at that moment, that a kinsman was on his way to find him—a brother he had possibly never before met, heading for a rendezvous planned and carried out by God.

'Providence' was a doctrine beloved of the Puritans and much reflected on by Christian scholars in the Middle Ages. It has not been a major concern of Christians in more modern times, however, who are sceptical of a view of God which implies that he organizes events like a chess player, moving pieces around the board of history to fit in with his hidden wisdom. We are certainly more at home with a God who responds rather than a God who preordains.

Yet any concept of an eternal, all-knowing, wise and good God surely requires some notion of 'providence', in the sense that complete knowledge allied to infinite power implies the ability to shape as well as to respond to events. To believe less is to reduce God to a detached observer of things, rather like the watchmaker who sets the new clock ticking but then simply leaves it to run its course.

That is not the God of the Bible and certainly not the God of the Exodus. He sees and feels, it is true, but he also acts. And in that action he operates both within and beyond our human understanding of time. He invited Moses and Aaron to share in his purposes. That was their privilege and would be their responsibility, but the plan and purpose were God's, not theirs.

A reflection

Many people have no problem with belief in a God who is simply the First Cause, who brought things into being. For them, 'God' is a remote, passionless being, not at all involved in our daily lives now. But that is not the God of the Bible. He is a God who cares, who is in his very nature love—'God is love' (1 John 4:16). He is responsive to prayer and active in history, both in its broad pattern and in its intimate detail. That is not at all to say that he is the immediate cause of every single event, for in that case he would be responsible for sin and injustice. Nor does he lightly intervene in the natural course of events, such as old age or illness, which are simply part of the world as it is.

What he does do is care—not just in a detached way, but in an involvement in the situation. This is the universal testimony of believers down the ages and the reason that we pray. He cares, he responds and he acts—not always in the way we would have chosen, but in a way that reveals his nature. Moses, and eventually the people of Israel, learnt much about God from what was to happen to them. So may we, as we pray and respond to his promptings.

RETURN TO EGYPT

EXODUS 4:18–31

When they heard that the Lord had given heed to the Israelites and that he had seen their misery, they bowed down and worshipped (v. 31).

Moses was torn between many emotions as he prepared to do what God had commanded him. It was a relief to be assured that those who had threatened his life were now dead—the Pharaoh who was effectively his grandfather, presumably, and his immediate court. But clearly he was racked with doubts about this strange mission. How would the Hebrew elders receive him? After all, his last encounter with his own people had not been a happy one. Would they really believe that he had been sent to them by God, even if the strange 'signs' he had been promised all worked perfectly? And how would they regard his new family of Midianites? All through the years of slavery, the one thing the people of his own race had done was to keep themselves clear of mixed marriages. But the one now presenting himself as their God-given saviour had 'married out' and compromised the integrity of the race.

Yet Moses set off, sent on his way with his father-in-law Jethro's blessing, and accompanied by his wife Zipporah and young sons. On the journey a strange encounter took place in the middle of the night, an event not unlike one that had befallen his ancestor Jacob when he had wrestled all night with an 'angel' (Genesis 32:24–26).

Moses experienced some kind of spiritual onslaught which at one point seemed likely to kill him. However, Zipporah, perhaps sensing that it was the inner conflict over racial and religious identity that was the source of the attack, found a sharp flintstone and with it circumcised her little son, touching Moses' 'feet' (possibly a euphemism for his penis) with the severed foreskin. Moses began to recover at once, perhaps deeply relieved that his wife had accepted their place as a family in the covenant that God had made with his ancestor Abraham, which was marked by the circumcision of every male infant. At this point, Zipporah and Moses' sons disappear from the scene, reappearing later in the story when Jethro brings them to meet Moses in Sinai.

When Moses reached the Sinai region, he was delighted to meet his brother Aaron, who had gone into the desert at God's prompting for this very purpose. They embraced, and Moses was able to tell him in detail what had happened at the burning bush and why he was now on his way back to Egypt. Relieved, perhaps, finally to have Aaron as his mouthpiece, Moses led the way back to Gershon, where he called for a meeting of the Hebrew elders.

It was an emotional gathering. Aaron recited all that Moses had been told and all that God had promised to do for them. He and Moses also showed them the 'signs' that God had given them—the staff becoming a snake and the apparently leprous hand instantly made whole. The elders were convinced. More than that, realizing that this was at last the answer to the cries and prayers that they had been making to the Lord, they bowed low to the earth and offered him their worship.

To achieve anything in life, great or small, we need goals, but we also need a degree of inner commitment to the task. At the burning bush, God had set the goals for Moses. It's hard to imagine a more daunting prospect than to tackle head-on the ruler of the world's greatest power, challenging him to let a tribe of useful slaves go free. Did Moses have the inner commitment, the strength of will, to do it? Perhaps it was the need to clarify that which lay behind the strange incident of his son's circumcision. Was Moses any longer truly and unambiguously part of the covenant people of God, or had he stepped outside that boundary when he decided to flee from Egypt? His wife seems to have settled the issue for him, just as the arrival of Aaron seems to have settled the equally daunting matter of his own supposed inadequacy for the task. Certainly, by the time he and his brother arrive in Egypt, we are beginning to sense a new Moses, a man who is showing personal courage, a focused determination and total commitment to the purpose of God.

A reflection

Though usually in a less dramatic way, the issues facing Moses face each of us when we set ourselves (or are set by others) new and daunting tasks. We too need to know that we are committed to them in an unambiguous way, that there is a goal to be reached and that we are wholehearted in our determination to reach it. For the Christian, as for Moses, there is of course the 'added factor', which is God's promise and presence. 'The one who calls you is faithful, and he will do this' (1 Thessalonians 5:24).

PHARAOH—THE FIRST ENCOUNTER

EXODUS 5:1–23

Moses and Aaron went to Pharaoh and said, 'Thus says the Lord, the God of Israel, "Let my people go, so that they may celebrate a festival to me in the wilderness."' But Pharaoh said, 'Who is the Lord, that I should heed him and let Israel go? I do not know the Lord, and I will not let Israel go' (vv. 1–2).

The story is presented here as a first meeting between the main protagonists followed by its painful consequences for the Hebrews. It is a process we shall see repeated several times—confrontation, rejection, disappointment. In this initial encounter, Pharaoh could hardly have been more dismissive, claiming that he had no knowledge of any 'God of Israel' and certainly didn't recognize that God's authority over any of his subjects. Moses and Aaron knew what they had been told by God to do and may (not unreasonably) have assumed that, with his help, their mission would be an instant success. After all, the Lord God Almighty had called them. All Pharaoh had were the shadowy gods of the underworld, who haunted the temples and tombs on the side of the setting sun.

So their first words to the king were confident and peremptory: 'Thus says the Lord, the God of Israel. "Let my people go, so that they may celebrate a festival to me in the wilderness."' The request—

perhaps 'demand' would be a better word—was absolutely clear.

And so was Pharaoh's response, which was brief and to the point. He posed one question, heavy with scepticism: 'Who is the Lord, that I should heed him?' He followed this with two daunting negatives: 'I do not know the Lord, and I will not let Israel go.'

Moses and Aaron, armed with the call and promise of God, and backed up by the signs he had given them to perform, had probably not expected to be so summarily dismissed. After all, their request was, in contemporary terms, not an unreasonable one: 'Our religion requires us to go off for a while into the desert and offer sacrifices.' It was the kind of requirement Pharaoh would have recognized and which, on a good day, he might have regarded favourably.

Perhaps unwisely, Moses and Aaron then added a threat, though it was a threat of dire consequences for the Hebrews rather than the Egyptians. If they were not permitted to make this sacrificial pilgrimage into the desert, the Lord would 'fall upon them [that is, the Hebrews] with pestilence and sword' (v. 3). This was not at all, of course, what God had said, and it's interesting to wonder why Moses changed the script in this way. Perhaps he felt that there would be no loss of face for Pharaoh if he were to let the Hebrews go under such terms, rather than confronting him with the threat of plagues on the Egyptian people themselves.

Whatever the reason, it didn't work. The king's interpretation of their behaviour was that he had been too lenient and allowed this tribe of slaves to have too much leisure, which they had apparently spent conceiving and bearing children. Now, he claimed, they were set to outnumber the bona fide residents of the land. Obviously they were finding the work insufficiently demanding, if they could talk of disappearing on a jaunt into the countryside for a few days. So he would make it harder. In future, the pieces of straw used in making the building bricks (presumably to hold the clay together) would not be provided for them. In other words, as well as making the bricks, the Hebrews would have to gather the bits of straw—quite a time-consuming process, but no extra time was to be allowed. More work, and less time to do it: that was the only apparent consequence of the visit by God's ambassadors to the court of Pharaoh.

Pharaoh's instruction was given to the Egyptian taskmasters, who passed it on to the Hebrew supervisors, presumably chosen for the task because they could speak the slaves' language. The news caused instant gloom to fall over the slave encampments. The work was arduous enough already; now it would be intolerable.

The supervisors (probably the elders of the people) went to Pharaoh themselves to plead their case. When he would hear none of it, they turned their anger and disappointment on Moses and Aaron. Suddenly, conditions that were previously bad enough appeared even worse in the light of these new measures. Why did Moses and Aaron ever broach their daft scheme or imagine that the most powerful ruler on earth would give way to the threats of two apparently powerless individuals? They forgot their earlier prayers, and the appearance on the scene of the two brothers, sent—they had claimed—by God himself in answer to their prayers. For the first but certainly not the last time, they turned on Moses and Aaron with bitter complaints: 'What have you done to us? All you have achieved is to give Pharaoh an excuse to kill us.'

Faced with their anger, Moses also sought a scapegoat—the Lord himself. His questions were truly bitter. 'Why?' he cried. 'Why have you mistreated your people—the people you said you planned to free? And why did you ever send me? Look, from the moment I first confronted Pharaoh it has brought nothing but trouble, and we are not an inch nearer delivering your people from bondage.'

Such words were to become something of a theme all through the story—both the complaints of the people, for whom blessings never came fast enough, and the frustration of Moses, whose faith seemed at times to hang on a very slender thread.

A reflection

It isn't hard for most of us to sympathize with the feelings both of the elders and of Moses. All through life we struggle to learn the gift of patience, but it is not easily acquired. In the modern world, especially, we are accustomed to instant gratification: as the credit card slogan used to say, 'Access takes the waiting out of wanting.' For the Christian believer there is also the tension between a fundamental faith that God will bring about his purpose in his own time, and our longing to see it now. 'Your kingdom come,' we pray, but deep down we don't expect to see it. To be told to 'wait' is probably the most irritating of all commands, whether it's in a queue or for a hospital appointment. 'Blessing now' *has often been the watchword of revivalist movements, but actually it must always be 'blessing* then'—*at the moment God has chosen, because it is the only right one.*

THE HARDENED HEART

EXODUS 7:1–25

Then the Lord said to Moses, 'Pharaoh's heart is hardened; he refuses to let the people go' (v. 14).

This is the first act of a drama played out in the court of the Egyptian king, the opening of what turned into a long duel between Moses, demanding that his people be allowed to go off into the desert, and a suspicious Pharaoh. Eventually this opening confrontation culminated in the first of a number of plagues to afflict the land—the turning of the waters of the Nile into 'blood'. As on each subsequent occasion, the king resisted Moses' demands, though not without moments of hesitation.

After the first rebuff, Moses and Aaron were commanded by God to go back to Pharaoh, though, strangely enough, with a clear warning that Pharaoh wouldn't listen to them. On their first visit they performed the 'signs' with Aaron's rod—he threw it to the ground and it turned into a snake. As the Lord had predicted, the Egyptian magicians, hurriedly summoned by the king, were able to do the same with their sticks, although—in a rather neat touch—Aaron's snake swallowed all the others. However, Pharaoh was not impressed. He 'hardened his heart' and would not consider their request.

This is the first step in a process that the Lord had already predicted, once at the burning bush (4:21) and now again, on the eve of the actual contest: 'I will harden Pharaoh's heart' (7:3). Time and again in the course of this vivid narrative we are told that the Lord hardened Pharaoh's heart (see 7:13; 9:12; 10:1, 20, 27; 11:10; 14:8), or that Pharaoh hardened his own heart (8:15, 32; 9:34), or, in the passive voice, that 'Pharaoh's heart was hardened' (8:19; 9:7, 35). The implication of all this, certainly to a modern reader, is that Pharaoh was not a free agent but simply did what God had planned, for whatever obscure reason. His response was apparently pre-ordained, leaving him no choice but to oppose the will of God and, together with his nation, suffer the awful consequences.

That, however, is to read the story through the cultural conditioning of the 21st century, rather than in the context of the ancient world or of the Jewish understanding of an 'act of God'. In fact, the three different ways in which the 'hardening' of the king's heart is described may help to clarify this. Sometimes it is said that Pharaoh hardened his heart; sometimes that God hardened it; and sometimes that it 'was hardened'. But each describes the same event.

That Pharaoh resisted the request of Moses and Aaron is the 'event'. That is what happened. Now, in a Jewish understanding of things, nothing can happen anywhere or at any time without God. He is the Lord of time, history, people, events. The Israelites did not deduce from this that he was necessarily the immediate cause of the event, but that it must have happened within the sphere of his ultimate control, which is the world that exists. Men and women, because they are created in his image, have a God-like freedom to act, to make decisions, even decisions which are foolish, wrong or downright evil, but even those decisions do not, as it were, take God by surprise. That belief, alien as it may sound to 21st-century ears, is the essential air of the Hebrew scriptures.

In this case, it means that Pharaoh, as a human being, had a God-given right to do what was wrong—but even that wrong decision was ultimately under the control of God. Looking at it from inside the king's head, so to speak, he was deciding not to yield to these demands—he hardened his heart. To the spectator, the deduction was that his heart was hardened (for whatever cause). And from the divine perspective, the Lord had hardened his heart.

Nor is this as unjust as it might sound, put in such stark terms. If we think of Pharaoh as being like the clay with which the Hebrews had to make bricks, and God as the hot desert sun in the sky, we can see that the sun would harden the clay. But if a plate of butter were to be put out in that same sun, it would melt: the sun would not harden but soften it. The sun is the same in both cases, but it is working on different substances. One could say that the clay can't help being clay and the butter can't help being butter; and that is true. But one must add that the sun can't help being the sun! God must be God, and we must live in the world that he has created, subject to both its natural and its moral laws. In one important sense, it is up to each of us whether we 'melt' or 'harden' before the will of God. That was where Pharaoh was culpable.

That is what we might call the philosophical problem about this story, a problem that may trouble some people and not others. There is also for a modern reader a problem in the actual narrative—all of these magic tricks, some of them performed at the behest of God and some by the skill of the Egyptian magicians. We may be able to accept that God would give Moses and Aaron the ability to perform such signs in the interests of liberating his people (though even there the flavour of folklore is not far away), but perhaps we balk at the idea that Pharaoh's magicians could do it, even to the extent of turning sticks into snakes or, a little later, the Nile into blood (7:22).

It is hard for us, with our secular, sceptical and scientific world-view, to breathe the air of this world of more than 3,000 years ago. Both the Egyptians and the Hebrews lived in a society where sorcery, magic, the black arts and supernatural events were taken for granted. This didn't mean that people weren't amazed by them, but it did mean that such things were not seen as beyond the world of reality. Even today, our modern folklore—what we tend to call 'modern myths'—abounds with such stories, partly because we enjoy them, in a strange kind of way, and partly because they induce a sense of awe and wonder that is lacking in cold rationality. In the ancient world, a god who could not bring about such events was not worth the title. To put it crudely, that's what gods were for.

This is not to propose that Moses and Aaron indulged either in conjuring tricks or in sorcery. Rather, it's to argue that Pharaoh—given his worldview, and that of his courtiers—would be unlikely to give heed to a couple of men making extravagant demands if they could not even equal the feats of his palace magicians. In the event, and, as the chronicler of Exodus sees it, by the will and power of Yahweh, they were able to exceed them—though even that, as it happened, was not enough to bend the will of the king.

Such questions did not trouble our storyteller, nor need they trouble us as we follow the unfolding narrative of a contest between dark and light, good and evil, justice and slavery. Of course the Judge of all the earth will be active for what is right and true; of course his power is greater than that of the false gods of the Nile; and of course those he calls to fulfil his purpose will in the end emerge as the victors. That is the story of Pharaoh, Moses and the plagues of Egypt in a nutshell.

A reflection

For Christians, 'signs' are ways in which God speaks to us, revealing truth or encouraging faith. That is how John's Gospel sees the miracles of Jesus: they are always called 'signs', by which God confirmed the ministry of Jesus to those who had eyes and faith to see them. Once or twice in my life—and most powerfully in one instance soon after my wife's death—I have experienced such a sign. I am not willing to describe it and I can't explain it, but I was left in no doubt that a perfectly 'ordinary' thing, in one sense, was in fact for me a sign or message from God. Moses and Aaron carried their rather more exotic signs into Pharaoh's palace and performed them as they had been told. But the king had no faith with which to see their true significance. His eyes were shut to their truth, and his heart was hardened. To see God's signs, our spiritual eyes must be opened, and that itself is a work of God (see, for instance, the two disciples in the home at Emmaus, Luke 24:30–31).

THE PLAGUES

EXODUS 8:1–32

But when Pharaoh saw that there was a respite, he hardened his heart, and would not listen to them (v. 15).

The first plague of Egypt was the only one that the Egyptian magicians managed to replicate. Moses and Aaron were told to confront Pharaoh as he went out to the water, to warn him of the danger of not responding to their demands and to tell him that with the staff in Moses' hand—the same one that had been turned into a snake a few days before—the Nile waters would be turned to blood. When he did exactly that, the water did indeed turn blood red—obviously not into literal blood, or the Egyptians would not have been able to drink the water after it had been filtered through the earth to the emergency wells that they had to dig (7:24). However, the king sent for his magicians and they, too, were able to turn water into 'blood', presumably in bowls or basins, and he scornfully rejected the request of Moses and Aaron: 'his heart remained hardened' (7:22).

From that point on, the plagues mounted in severity and it is significant that the magicians were unable to replicate them. Indeed, after the plague of frogs (8:1–15) turned into a plague of gnats (8:16–18)—quite a logical sequence, given the presence of piles of dead frogs throughout the land—the magicians failed to produce gnats by their secret arts, and even confessed to Pharaoh, 'This is the finger of God!' (8:19). However, the plagues, and even the words of his magicians, failed to persuade Pharaoh: 'he would not listen to them, just as the Lord had said'. Indeed, he was rather more culpable than that, because he took any sign of mercy or respite on God's part as evidence of weakness: 'When Pharaoh saw that there was a respite, he hardened his heart' (8:15).

The plague of gnats was followed in due course by a plague of flies (8:20–24). Moses warned that 'the houses of the Egyptians shall be filled with swarms of flies'—indeed, the whole land of Egypt would be filled with them except Goshen, where the Israelites had their settlements. In the event, the flies came into the house of Pharaoh and into his officials' houses. Perhaps for the first time, one of the plagues affected him personally.

Whatever the reason, Pharaoh began to weaken his resistance. He sent for Moses and said that they could go to offer their sacrifices to God, but only within the borders of Egypt. Moses rejected this compromise position out of hand. The Egyptian people would find the Hebrew sacrifices offensive and turn on them. No, they must go a three-day journey into the wilderness and there offer the sacrifices God had commanded.

Not for the first time in history, a bully challenged turned into a bully trying to find a way out. 'All right,' Pharaoh said in effect, 'you may go, provided you don't go very far away.' Then he added, surprisingly, 'Pray for me' (v. 28). He may have meant no more than that Moses should pray for the plague of flies to be called off, which Moses promptly promised to do. Yet the simple words seem to suggest more—that here was a man who in his heart of hearts knew that he had been challenging a greater power than that of a human ruler, or even of the gods of Egypt, and suddenly felt vulnerable. If so, it is a rare insight into the humanity of the most powerful man in the ancient world.

Moses did exactly what he was asked. He 'went out from Pharaoh and prayed to the Lord' (v. 30). As a result, the swarms of flies were removed. But as soon as they were, presumably taking this as a sign of weakness or softening on Moses' part, Pharaoh withdrew his permission for the Israelites to go off into the wilderness. 'Pharaoh hardened his heart this time also, and would not let the people go' (v.32).

In the heart and mind of Pharaoh we can sense that a battle was being fought, and it is one with which we are all uncomfortably familiar. It was a battle between his own will—the will of a hard, arrogant man who was used to getting his own way—and the will of God. As he swung between the two, he exhibited an indecisiveness that he would have despised in others. Should he let the wretched Hebrews go? By now, he must have realized, they were more trouble than they were worth as slave labour. It would take only a word, and they would be gone for ever. Yet to say that word would lead to a public loss of face, and a private admission that there was a power at work here that was greater than the power of imperial Egypt. So sometimes he spoke the word, especially when he thought that it would bring respite from the plagues, but the word was always rescinded when the immediate pressure was relaxed and he could fool himself that perhaps it would never return.

A reflection

This is a picture of a struggle that is familiar to most of us, the struggle between conscience and self. Like Pharaoh, when the pressure is on we are apt to make promises. 'Get me out of this, Lord, and I will give myself unstintingly to your service.' But when the respite comes and better times take over, it is desperately easy to forget the promises we made. It is not only true of New Year resolutions or Lenten vows. Most of us have been guilty at some time or another of promising one thing and doing another, or of changing our moral stance when circumstances change. We may not like to think of that as 'hardening our hearts', but in truth that is what it is.

THE FINAL TEST

EXODUS 9:1—10:29

Then Pharaoh said to Moses, 'Get away from me! Take care that you do not see my face again, for on the day you see my face you shall die.' Moses said, 'Just as you say! I will never see your face again' (vv. 28–29).

Inevitably, the battle between Moses and Pharaoh escalated. Moses could see that the king was weakening under the constant barrage of plagues, and in fact some of his own officials were beginning to fault his leadership. 'Let the people go,' they argued, 'so that they may worship the Lord their God; do you not yet understand that Egypt is ruined?' (10:7).

This complaint followed the devastating hail, which in turn followed an epidemic of sickness among the cattle and a widespread outbreak of boils on humans and animals. As one plague followed another, each in its way natural enough but cumulatively a disaster of catastrophic proportions, it was not surprising that opposition to Pharaoh's hard line would begin to grow. Even he had begun to make certain offers to Moses and Aaron—that the people could go, but not very far; or that they could go but leave their children behind, or their cattle. Clearly he had some doubt as to whether they ever intended to return and wanted a kind of deposit of value to ensure that they did.

By now Moses could scent victory. His demand became nothing

less than unconditional surrender. The Israelites must be allowed to go, with wives, children and cattle. As he put it very graphically, 'Not a hoof shall be left behind' (10:26). Sensing victory, he was not prepared to accept half measures, and from his manner Pharaoh must have deduced that much more than a brief journey into the wilderness to offer sacrifices to the Lord was at stake.

If these accounts of the plagues were taken literally, one could be forgiven for wondering how the Egyptians survived at all. All the Egyptian livestock (but none of the Hebrew) are described as killed by the plague of cattle sickness (9:6), yet Egyptian livestock also perished in numbers during the subsequent hailstorm (9:19–21). This is, of course, typical of the language of storytelling, which is imprecise in detail but vivid in impact. Throughout these narratives, it is obvious that words like 'all' and 'every' are not necessarily being used in their literal sense—perhaps 'many' would be a simpler version. But in any case, what mattered was the effect of the plagues. Slowly, through event after event, the will of Pharaoh, that proud and powerful king, was being put to the test.

It's reasonable to wonder why. Why did God propose an escalating series of disasters, instead of going straight through to the final plague that brought about the release of the Hebrews? What was gained by the long cat-and-mouse process? An answer—and a very Jewish answer, at that—is given immediately before the penultimate plagues, the locusts and then the darkness. 'The Lord said to Moses, "Go to Pharaoh, for I have hardened his heart and the heart of his officials, in order that I might show these signs of mine among them. and that you may tell your children and grandchildren how I have made fools of the Egyptians and what signs I have done among them—so that you may know that I am the Lord"' (10:1–2).

Here is a double witness—to the Egyptian leaders, in the hope that they might even at this late hour soften their hard hearts and submit to God's will; and to the Hebrews, so that they would know that the God of the Hebrews is 'the Lord', Yahweh, the eternal 'I Am'.

Quite apart from the fascinating detail of the story, there is here an eternal question, often posed and seldom answered. Why does

God delay his justice? It is the treatment of that question which makes this story much more than a simple narrative about a wicked king and a determined liberator. In fact, the whole process was necessary both for the Egyptians and the Israelites.

For the Israelites, it was a lesson in salvation, a lesson to be repeated and commemorated for ever. They could not save themselves from the power of Egypt, but their God, Yahweh, could and would do it. They had cried to him for help, and this was the way the help was to come. The whole narrative, with its struggles, doubts and setbacks, was a learning process they would forget at their peril.

For the Egyptians, these repeated opportunities for repentance, for submission to the will and justice of God, remove all excuse. Pharaoh knew—every word of dialogue hints at the invisible process —that he could not defeat this strange, powerful and invisible God of the Hebrews. He also knew that right and justice were on the side of the slaves. If he was to be finally condemned and judged, God— the 'Judge of all the earth'—would ensure that there was no injustice in the sentence or penalty. Time after time, through these signs, God was appealing to Pharaoh's conscience. It must be right to assume that at any point in the process this man, given (like all of us) the fearful right to choose, could have chosen to let the Hebrew slaves go. He would have lost face, it is true. The great Pharaoh might have been seen to be defeated by a bunch of uncultured yokels. But the offer was there, as some of his own officials could see, and it was folly upon folly to reject it out of hand.

Yet that was what he did. Pride is a strange and often destructive force. Rather than lose face—be 'made a fool of', as Exodus puts it (10:2)—he was prepared to bring about devastation for his country and, in the end, tragedy for himself and his household. The scene is brought to an abrupt conclusion with his blunt and dismissive words. If Moses insisted on going with all of his people, their cattle and their goods, then let him try it. Simply to present himself in Pharaoh's court again would be to invite his death. There could be no more dialogue, no compromise, no negotiation.

Moses took his words and threw them back in his face. It would indeed be as Pharaoh had said. They would never approach him again. The moment of decision had come.

A reflection

What this part of the story tells us is that freedom has a price. It is seldom lightly achieved, whether it is freedom from physical oppression (such as the apartheid regime in South Africa twenty years ago) or the oppression of circumstances, emotions or sins. In many ways the whole story of the Bible is the story of liberation, from the moment that Adam and Eve lost their innocence, and hence their freedom, in the Garden of Eden, to the coming of the Saviour who said that if he set us free, we would be 'free indeed'—truly and eternally free (John 8:36). Here, in Egypt, the price of freedom was paid by the Lord, but it also involved much human suffering, tears and tragedy. In the 'Egypts' that each of us inhabit, there is also very often a slavery. Perhaps the One who longs to set the captives free is waiting for that 'cry' that reached the ears of God over 3,000 years ago.

THE TRAGIC REFUSAL

EXODUS 11:1–10

The Lord gave the people favour in the sight of the Egyptians (v. 3).

When Moses came back from the desert and first presented himself at Pharaoh's court, it's interesting to speculate how he would have been received. Presumably some people, at least, remembered him, the young Hebrew who grew up in the household of the princess and then mysteriously disappeared. Moses would have spoken Egyptian fluently, of course, and been familiar with the culture, idiom and religion of the land.

Yet from the first, his meetings with Pharaoh were confrontational. Moses made demands; the king rejected them. The demands turned into threats and the threats into events, with a succession of plagues inflicted on the Egyptian people. With occasional moments of indecision, Pharaoh held firm, even when his officials argued that the damage already done to the land and its people far outweighed the economic value to them of the Hebrew slaves. Clearly, between Moses and the king there was a personal animosity which made rational responses by Pharaoh difficult. Finally, as we have seen, they broke off all relationship. Moses would be put to death if he presented himself again at the palace, and he promised that he would never see Pharaoh's face again.

Outside that private confrontation, it would seem that over the intervening weeks Moses had become a figure of power in the land.

Presumably people knew that he was the source of all these threats of plague and also that he seemed to be able to call them off by addressing his God. The Egyptian people began to look with new respect at their Hebrew neighbours. Perhaps they were not such a bunch of helpless slaves after all. Whatever Pharaoh thought about it, 'the Lord gave the people favour in the sight of the Egyptians. Moreover, Moses himself was a man of great importance in the land of Egypt, in the sight of Pharaoh's officials and in the sight of the people' (11:3).

This is the setting for the final and most devastating plague, the death of the firstborn sons of Egypt. In preparation for it, the Hebrews were to ask their Egyptian neighbours for 'articles of silver and gold' (12:35), presumably with some suggestion that to hand them over would lessen the impact of what was to come. The articles themselves would prove useful as bribes or payments for food on the proposed desert journey.

Moses—'hot with anger' (11:8), and apparently disregarding both Pharaoh's warning and his own promise on a last visit to the palace— spelt out for Pharaoh's benefit the precise nature of the threat he was making. The firstborn son of every family, from the highest in the land to the lowliest, would die, yet not a single Israelite would be harmed, 'so that you may know that the Lord makes a distinction between Egypt and Israel' (11:7). Pharaoh was not impressed. In the language of Exodus, 'the Lord hardened his heart', an outcome foretold by God 'in order that my wonders may be multiplied in the land of Egypt' (11:9).

It's useless to raise questions here about the morality of such a judgment, simply because the ancient and modern worldviews are incapable of communicating with each other on such an issue. Pharaoh was stubborn, angry and determined, we would say. He was not going to be outwitted by a bunch of slaves and their upstart leader. Those were the observable facts of the matter. If one believed, as probably in rather different ways both Israelite and Egyptian did, that everything that happened was ordained by divine decree, that is only a different way of saying that God made Pharaoh stubborn, angry and determined. God's purpose was to bring the Hebrews out of Egypt, and the person who stood in the way of that was the Egyptian king. Whatever was necessary to achieve the divine purpose had to take place.

It is also a modern problem to wonder about the justice of the slaughter of a huge number of innocent children, or to be appalled by the sorrow and bereavement that flowed from it in homes all over the land. On the contrary, the chronicler of Exodus seems to relish the thought: 'there will be a loud wailing throughout the whole land of Egypt—such as has never been or will ever be again' (11:6). Here, he would say, the divine will must prevail. The Egyptians had been given many opportunities to release their slaves. Many less dreadful plagues had already given them due warning of the consequences of hanging on to them. Individual guilt did not come into it: this was the guilt of a society under its imperial ruler. Pharaoh hardened his heart, but it was the young boys of Egypt who were to die.

In every situation of conflict there is a moment of crisis. The Greek word *krisis* from which our English word is derived means, quite simply, 'judgment' or 'choice'. A crisis is the moment of judgment, when the issues come to a head and are finally—even if only painfully—resolved. This final plague was the moment of crisis in the conflict between the Hebrew slaves, under their new leader Moses, and the powerful Egyptian state, under its powerful king. The scene was set both for the final tragedy of this confrontation and for the great deliverance that was to mark out the people of Israel for the rest of their history.

A reflection

Often in life we dread the moment of crisis, even praying for it to be delayed or avoided somehow. In fact, a crisis is often necessary to a proper outcome. Hiding or avoiding painful facts or elements in a situation seldom leads to true healing or justice. Here, the facts were plain enough. Justice was on the side of the slaves, as was God, who is the God of justice and mercy. The issue could have been resolved earlier, given goodwill on the part of Pharaoh, but obstinacy ('hardening of the heart') prevailed. Its consequences, as so often, were disastrous—not for his enemies, but for himself, his own family and his people. We are not called as God's people to create crises, but we are often called to face them as resolutely as Moses did, and with a similar faith in a God of justice and mercy, who 'executes judgment'.

THE PASSOVER

EXODUS 12:1–20

'This is how you shall eat it: your loins girded, your sandals on your feet, and your staff in your hand; and you shall eat it hurriedly. It is the passover of the Lord' (v. 11).

Obeying divine instructions, the Israelites were to prepare this strange 'last supper', which came to be known as Passover, from the Hebrew word *pesah*, to 'skip over'. The Lord promised that when he passed through the land of Egypt on that special night, to 'strike down every firstborn in the land of Egypt', he would 'skip over' the homes of the Israelites, marked by the lamb's blood on their doorposts. For the Hebrew people, carrying out these strange rituals was an act of faith, pure and simple, because, contrary to evidence and bitter experience, the whole assumption of what they were doing was that they were about to leave Egypt in a hurry, and for ever. Their recent experience of Pharaoh constantly changing his mind at the last moment was not enough to counter their communal sense of purpose and confidence in God—a confidence that depended to a large extent on their leader, Moses, who obviously now commanded enormous respect.

So they were to kill and prepare the lamb, daubing its blood on their doorposts. They were to bake unleavened bread, because there would be no time for a fermented loaf to rise. They were to put on their travelling garments and pack up their belongings. Then they must eat the meal, in their family groups, 'in haste', in the belief that there simply was no time for a more elaborate banquet to mark the end of their miserable sojourn in Egypt. It was a magnificent demonstration of faith, which would have looked pretty foolish in the cold light of dawn if once again Egyptian soldiers had barred their way.

This 'Passover' ritual was not to be a one-off event—far from it. For ever afterwards the Hebrew people were to remember it by an annual celebration—a 'day of remembrance'—in which they would once again share this meal and retell the ancient story of their ancestors' deliverance from slavery.

The idea behind the Hebrew word *zakar*, translated 'remembrance' (v. 14), is in fact difficult to express in English. It is certainly much more than just 'calling to mind', as we observe Remembrance Day to call to mind those who died in the wars of the last century. The word *zakar* is seldom used of a purely cerebral activity, just 'remembering'. It carries the sense of a past action made real today —but not 'repeated', because obviously the Passover event was unique in itself. As Jewish people celebrate it today, they place its events in the present rather than the past: 'you brought *us* out of bondage in Egypt'. This single event is placed every year right in the centre of people's ordinary lives and observed as the mighty deed of God that brought the nation into existence. It is 'remembered' and, in the act of remembering, something happens.

So here the people are given instructions not only for this first Passover but for an annual event, to be carried on as a 'perpetual ordinance' (12:14). And so it has been, as Jewish people all over the world gather in their families for the meal and for the recital of the story of that foundational event in their history. Long centuries after the temple has ceased to exist, this ordinance is still observed, probably the one Jewish festival that even the least 'religious' Jews continue to observe.

It is also known as the 'Festival of Unleavened Bread', because for seven days every Jewish home is to be free from any trace of leaven (yeast), and the only bread eaten is *matzos*, the approved unleavened biscuit. By one of those strange connections of religious practice, the leaven—simply an innocent ingredient, to be omitted on the first Passover night because there was no time for bread to rise—became a symbol of infectious evil, an idea so deeply rooted in Jewish thought that Jesus used it as a metaphor to describe the corrupting effect of the hypocrisy of the scribes and Pharisees of his time (see, for example, Matthew 16:6).

It's hard to imagine the people's feelings as they received their instructions. Were they really going to leave Egypt, the only home-land any of them had ever known, to head off across the desert for an unknown destination? It's not clear whether at this moment Moses had told them where they were to go, though it was soon revealed to them that it was the land of the Canaanites, Hittites, Amorites, Hivites and Jebusites, the present occupants of the land in which Abraham had settled after leaving Ur of the Chaldees. Perhaps at that moment it was judged enough of a trauma for the people to manage the flight from Egypt, without the burden of knowing that at the end of their journey they would have to fight for space in an already populated land.

For Moses and Aaron, of course, there was the utter conviction of God's call, confirmed, as we might say, by 'signs following'—the burning bush, the plagues, and now this last and most terrible judgment on the land of Egypt and its stubborn ruler. For the people, it was to be a massive act of faith. Could it really be, as Moses was saying, that they would actually leave in safety, with the encourage-ment of the Egyptian people, and without having to raise so much as a single sword to achieve it?

A reflection

To understand what happens at Passover helps Christians to understand more clearly what happens in Holy Communion, the Eucharist, which of course was instituted by Jesus in the context of the Passover rituals. In the Jewish Mishnah (the written version of the Torah, the Law) it says that every person in each generation should think of themselves as personally coming out of Egypt: 'Therefore it was not only our ancestors whom the Holy One, blessed is he, redeemed from slavery. We were also redeemed together with them.' In the same way, Christians 'remember' the sacrifice by which Jesus set us free and won for us eternal life, but not simply as an event in the remote past that happened to other people. His action, unrepeated and unrepeatable as it is, is nevertheless effective right now for us who live 20 centuries later.

The other cause for reflection is, surely, the enormous faith that this event demanded of the ordinary Israelites. They really were being invited to take a long journey into the unknown, solely (in human terms) on the words of Moses and Aaron. Not only that, but experience had told them how often past hopes of escape had been dashed. Yet they believed God and were ready to set out on this strange and terrifying expedition. As a communal act of faith it is probably unparalleled in human history. That, in itself, is a challenge to the faith of present-day Christians. To trust in God alone and stake everything on him is the very model of a living faith.

THE END OF
THE BEGINNING

EXODUS 12:21–50

'Rise up, go away from my people, both you and the Israelites! Go, worship the Lord, as you said. Take your flocks and herds, as you said, and be gone. And bring a blessing on me, too!' (vv. 31–32).

At midnight, it happened. The narrator struggles to put the event into words. 'The Lord struck down all the firstborn in the land of Egypt' (v. 29). 'The Lord will pass through to strike down the Egyptians... and will not allow the destroyer to enter your houses' (v. 23). It was the Lord, or this mysterious 'destroyer' as his agent, who went about this awesome task. There was not a house without someone dead. Pharaoh's eldest son died, but so, we are told, did the firstborn of the prisoner in the dungeon (v. 29). It was an apocalyptic event—the consequence of the king's cruelty and stubbornness, of course, but wreaking pain, anguish and tears on every Egyptian household without distinction. To the modern reader, it is a tragic conclusion to the struggle for liberation, but to the oppressed Hebrews it was the 'night of nights'.

In the morning, at first light, they left, an endless column of men, women, children, cattle and carts, making their way towards Succoth to the east. They carried with them jewellery, gold, silver and clothes, pressed on them by Egyptian neighbours desperate that they should leave before further disaster fell on them. They also carried the unleavened dough, suggesting that Moses' statement that they would eat only unleavened bread was more a statement of what would happen than a command to be obeyed. The dough was carried on the shoulders of the people in cloaks and baked into cakes when they stopped for an alfresco meal on the first day of their journey.

The narrator tells us that the Hebrews had lived in Egypt 430 years, which means that the history of the clan before the settlement would have been a very distant memory indeed. Egypt, for better or worse, had been their home—at first a place of refuge during a severe famine, then a new land of opportunity under friendly rule, and finally a place of slavery under a cruel king. The original descendants of Jacob had, of course, multiplied, even if the figure of 600,000 men, besides children, seems unlikely. Precise numbers were not a strong point in the ancient world, but there is no doubt that the chronicler intends to convey the picture of a great multitude making its way out of Goshen towards the desert.

Again the rules for the observance of the Passover are rehearsed. The previous night had been observed as a night of vigil for the Lord. Now every Passover night was to be similarly observed, though only and strictly by those who had been circumcised, whether they were of Hebrew or alien birth. Presumably this regulation permitted the wives of circumcised males to eat the Passover, because there is no doubt that whole families shared in this annual celebration, as they still do today.

As the people made their way out of Egypt, the air behind them echoing with the cries of mourning yet with the gifts of the Egyptian people in their hands, it is hard to imagine the feelings of the Israelites. They were leaving a land of slavery, and that was a fact. But what lay ahead for them? There was uninviting desert and scrubland to cross, hills and mountains in the distance, the waters of the Reed Sea ahead of them and any number of hostile tribes ready to resist any incursion on to their lands. Even in slavery there was some security, the familiarity of home and fireside, and the provision of food and water enough for their needs.

Perhaps some of them saw that this was but the first step towards a distant and unknown end, and human beings are not very good at coping with unknown ends. The wisest among them will have realized that this was not (in Winston Churchill's war-time saying) so much the beginning of the end as the end of the beginning.

Even a good and longed-for change can be traumatic. We speak of people becoming 'institutionalized' in hospitals or nursing homes, so that 'normal' life seems threatening and insecure. C.S. Lewis once said that he could stand anything so long as it was familiar! Yet here, in this great story of a people, the most massive and traumatic change took place literally overnight. Although it is true that Moses had promised that they would one day leave under the hand of God for a new life free from slavery, it would be hard to think of a more sudden and spectacular change in the destiny of a whole people than this one.

Many of them, of course, would have been sustained by a strong faith in the God of their fathers, and it is doubtful whether, without this, any of them would have embarked on what was humanly speaking a crazy adventure. How would such a vast multitude be fed in areas of the journey where there was no ready food to be gathered or even bought?

History records several comparable mass migrations—the Boers in South Africa, the American Indians from their tribal lands in the South under cruel compulsion, the Mormons on their long trek to Salt Lake City. None of them, either in numbers or the nature of the task, even begins to equal this one.

A reflection

At such moments of traumatic change in our lives, the decisive factor is normally what provides our spiritual undergirding. Even moving house can have devastating psychological side-effects, let alone bereavement, redundancy or a crippling accident. At least it can be said of Moses and Aaron, as they led this motley crowd out of Egypt, that they knew that they were doing it at the command and within the will and purpose of God. That was their spiritual undergirding—to be severely tested over the coming months and years, it is true, but nevertheless the supreme consolation on the brink of an awesome venture.

THE GUIDING PILLAR

EXODUS 13

The Lord went in front of them in a pillar of cloud by day, to lead them along the way, and in a pillar of fire by night, to give them light, so that they might travel by day and by night (v. 21).

Led by Moses and Aaron, and perhaps by the party of men carrying the bones of Joseph in a litter (Genesis 50:25), the vast emigration began, the crowd making its way eastward from Goshen. It's hardly surprising that there was a 'pillar of cloud by day', when one thinks of the thousands of feet and hooves disturbing the sandy terrain, and possibly the light of a thousand campfires at night created the pillar of fire. Of course the narrator intends much more than such a simple and down-to-earth explanation. This journey—indeed, their entire liberation from Egypt—was to be undertaken at God's initiative. He had brought them out and now he would lead the way, his presence symbolized by the cloud (a frequent image of the divine manifestation in the scriptures) and by the pillar of fire.

It's hard to think of a single such liberation in human history, achieved without the liberated having so much as to raise a sword or strike a blow. As the Jews have delighted to recall down the centuries, God brought them out solely by his own 'outstretched arm'. Their contribution was to trust him, no more and no less. Even their great leader, Moses, was no more than the assistant stage manager, as God produced and directed the entire event. It is doubtless hard for any of us to accept that we owe what we are entirely to the actions of another. Indeed, Christians have struggled with the whole concept of 'grace'—the undeserved favour of God—from the early days of the Church until now. It's as though we are desperate to bring something to our own salvation, or that it is in some sense demeaning to depend so utterly on someone else, even if that 'someone' is God.

Out from Egypt they came, delivered from slavery by the mighty acts of God and now led on their path towards the promised land by these 'pillars' of his presence. For the moment, trust was easy, but it was to be sorely tested soon enough. It was not to be just yet, however. 'God did not lead them by way of the land of the Philistines, although that was nearer; for God thought "If the people face war, they may change their minds and return to Egypt." So God led the people by the roundabout way of the wilderness toward the Red (or Reed) Sea' (13:17–18). They camped eventually at Etham, which is on the edge of the desert.

In the manner of generals all through history, Moses then addressed the people, calling on them to remember this day when they came out of slavery in Egypt, brought to freedom by the strength of God's hand. He also revealed to them their eventual destination, the 'land flowing with milk and honey', though at present occupied (they may have been disappointed to hear) by Canaanites, Hivites, Amorites, Hittites and Jebusites (v. 5). To mark their deliverance, they were to eat unleavened bread for the next seven days, which would in any case be days of constant and urgent travel, putting as much distance between themselves and the Egyptians as possible. And he reminded them that they were to keep this practice at the 'proper time' from year to year in the future (v. 10).

Moses also set out for them a principle which was to mark the religion of Israel to the present day, the 'consecration' of the firstborn male. Because their deliverance from slavery was brought about by the death of the firstborn sons of Egypt, while their own sons were kept safe, they and their successors were to be considered as 'consecrated'—set apart—for the Lord. Firstborn animals in their herds were to be killed and offered as sacrifices, but firstborn sons were to be 'redeemed' or 'bought back', by the offering of a sacrifice to the Lord (v. 15).

Over a thousand years later, when Jesus was born, Joseph and Mary took their baby boy to the temple to 'present him to the Lord' and to offer a simple sacrifice, in their case 'a pair of turtledoves or two young pigeons' (Luke 2:24)—the offering permitted for those too poor to afford a lamb or young goat. The offering was a recognition of the price of the redemption of God's people in the shedding of blood. They were never to take it lightly, or think that it was a deliverance without cost.

Not only that, but here also was the notion of a people 'purchased' by Yahweh to be his own. That was the other message of the great escape. God delivered them from Egypt for a clear and distinct purpose—to be his. They were not set free to do as they liked, but to become a people under his divine rule, a 'theocracy' in the pure sense of the word. The giving of the Law, later on in the journey, was a mark of this, but right from the start of this new adventure Moses was laying down the principles which would govern the community that had just come to birth. These first precepts—the eating of unleavened bread, the observance of the yearly Passover and the dedication of the firstborn—were binding on the people because their liberation had been the work of the Lord, Yahweh, alone. By it, he had made them his. Their obedience and faith had brought them this far under his hand. There would be no future for them anywhere else.

A reflection

The language that we find here about escape, redemption, liberation, sacrifice and ransom occurs repeatedly throughout the Old Testament, especially in the Psalms and the Hebrew prophets. It is also very much the language of the New Testament, familiar to Christians in a different context. Jesus is the new 'Moses' (there are 22 references in the Gospels and epistles to his role as God's saviour, redeemer and liberator of his people). He is worthy of 'more glory' than Moses, because Moses 'was faithful in God's house as a servant', whereas Jesus was 'faithful over God's house as a son' (Hebrews 3:3–6).

For the Christian, this narrative serves to remind us that our salvation, every bit as much as that of the Israelites of old, is dependent solely on the activity of God. We cannot free ourselves from the slavery of sin. We cannot, unaided, bring ourselves to the promised land. We are 'saved by grace, through faith' (Ephesians 2:8), just as they were. When we raise our voices and hands in triumphant praise, as they did on the road out of Egypt, we too need to remember whose triumph it is. To take our eyes off the pillar of cloud, or to rest in any other confidence than the pillar of fire, is to think that we can do it ourselves. As the people on the desert way were to discover, that is the worst of all possible mistakes.

ONE LAST HURDLE

EXODUS 14:1–9

'I will gain glory for myself over Pharaoh and all his army; and the Egyptians shall know that I am the Lord' (v. 4).

You might feel that the slaughter of the firstborn and the ignominious way in which the Egyptians let their slaves leave laden with treasure would be enough humble pie for Pharaoh and his people, but one final and devastating humiliation remains for the leader of the most powerful empire in the world. The chronicler of Exodus relishes every detail of the story, taking care to give every credit to Yahweh rather than to Moses, Aaron and the people of Israel.

If it all seems a bit too gloating for modern taste, we must try to see it in its context. The Hebrews had come into Egypt as little more than an extended family. They came at the express invitation of Pharaoh. Over the intervening years dwelling in Goshen, the land they had been allocated as a gift, they multiplied. Eventually they were enslaved by their erstwhile friends. Through the long years of slavery that followed, they had kept the religion of their fathers, prayed and longed for deliverance and finally welcomed two men who came, they claimed, at the direct behest of the God of Israel to bring about their release. With more generosity than one might have expected, these men—Moses and Aaron—gave the Egyptian king many opportunities to let the people go peacefully and without harm to anyone. These opportunities were spurned time and again, often with scornful words.

Put in that context, it is hardly surprising that the escaping slaves enjoyed the spectacle of the Egyptian king being humiliated and forced to let them go, still—as he made clear—against his will. As the chronicler saw it, he had simply been compelled to submit to the greater power of the Lord God of Israel. It was that power, his 'strong hand' (13:9), that had brought all this about, and it was right to celebrate his victory.

This final phase of the struggle for liberation (to put it in modern words) began with yet another *volte face* by Pharaoh. 'What have we done,' he asked his advisors, 'letting Israel leave our service?' (v. 5). It's unlikely that the economic loss of their slave labour weighed as heavily as the insult to the imperial power of Egypt, defied and finally outwitted by this tribe of slaves. To let them go would have been tantamount to an admission that their God was greater than the gods of the Nile, and their power greater than the king's.

So, for one last time, Pharaoh went back on his original decision to let them leave. He gathered a considerable military force, including the famed Egyptian charioteers, and ordered them to pursue the departing Hebrews, round them up and bring them back. To demonstrate the extent of his commitment to the expedition, Pharaoh had his own chariot prepared and intended to accompany his troops into the desert.

Meanwhile the Israelites had turned back from the direct path of escape and were camped in front of Baal-zephon, by the waters which barred further progress. Militarily speaking, this seemed a suicidal move, but Moses told the people that this was at the command of Yahweh, 'so that he would gain glory for himself over Pharaoh and all his army' (v. 4). The Egyptian king had defied the Lord God long enough. The moment of final reckoning was at hand.

Again the narrative speaks of the Lord 'hardening the heart' of Pharaoh, although on any ordinary human assessment it was, of course, Pharaoh who hardened his own heart. Indeed, we are even told the reason why he did it—out of frustration and anger that the

Israelites had escaped so triumphantly from his clutches. But the chronicler is determined to ensure that the Lord, and the Lord alone, is seen as the originator, orchestrator and executor of the whole process.

The Hebrews, we are told, were going out 'boldly' (v. 8), though perhaps a little surprised at Moses's insistence that they make camp on the enemy side of the sea. Yet even here there was a stratagem involved. As the narrative records, the king would hear reports of their encampment and assume that they were effectively trapped by the wilderness on one side, and the sea on the other, and reduced to 'wandering aimlessly' (v. 3). This would serve to encourage him to pursue them, as they were still well within range of his chariots and horsemen.

The decision was made. The army of Pharaoh set out, heading towards the Israelites in their vast camp on the edge of what most experts now think was not the Red but the Reed Sea. The Hebrew name is *yam sup*, or 'Sea of Reeds'. This was an area of water to the north of the Red Sea which was relatively shallow. It's an area through which the present-day Suez Canal was built. They were indeed trapped, because the desert led back to Egypt and the oncoming Egyptians, and ahead was the equivalent of a shallow lake, quite impossible for this assorted horde of young and old, fit and infirm, men and women to be able to cross together.

Probably wisely, Moses waited for the people's response to manifest itself. It was at his command that they had halted their flight and pitched camp between the borders of Egypt and the Reed Sea ahead of them, rather than pressing on while they could. After all, he had done it at the express command of the Lord (v. 1), who had revealed to him the purpose behind what seemed to be an irrational and risky move. For the present, the people were not to know, but inevitably the moment would come when they would demand answers and explanations. Not for the first time, the moment of crisis—that is, danger plus opportunity—was facing them.

A reflection

We all know the feeling. We've made a momentous decision, taken a huge step forward—and then suddenly panic grips us. Has it all been a mistake? We feel trapped, because realistically we can't go back (we burnt our bridges, as it were) and at the moment we can't go forward either. Add to that, as there was in this case, some overwhelming power at our heels— a destructive force waiting to pounce on our indecision—and the case seems desperate.

It probably would not have helped the Israelites to be told, at this moment, that God was actually at work on their behalf to humiliate and destroy the obstinate king of Egypt and to bring them eventually to the promised land. Equally, of course, we might well find it irritating or irrelevant of people to tell us, when we feel trapped between the danger behind and the challenge ahead, that 'God intended it for good' (Genesis 50:20). In the end, however, faith is confidence that in all circumstances we are in God's hands.

FREE AT LAST

EXODUS 14:10–31

Israel saw the great work that the Lord did against the Egyptians. So the people feared the Lord and believed in the Lord and in his servant Moses (v. 31).

The crisis came quickly, in fact as soon as the people in the camps could see gathering on the horizon an army of Egyptian soldiers and chariots. All of a sudden it didn't seem such a good idea to have taken on the might of the world's most powerful nation. This wasn't what Moses had promised them. As often in such circumstances, they had an attack of selective memory. They recalled telling Moses —perhaps when he first appeared from the desert—to 'leave them alone and let them serve the Egyptians' (v. 12), though no such request had been recorded by the chronicler. Looking at the choices before them—drowning in the Sea of Reeds or being slaughtered by the Egyptians—they argued, not unreasonably, that they would have been better off in Egypt, though still slaves, of course.

Moses had stern and bold words for them. This was not to be by any means the last time that the people would complain in these terms, but he must have been somewhat dismayed that their faith was proving so weak at the first challenge to it. 'Don't be afraid,' he told them. 'Stand firm... The Lord will fight for you, and you have only to keep still' (vv. 13–14). Presumably this confidence was based on his conviction that all that had happened had been in response to what he understood to be God's clear commands. The God of their fathers, whom he had encountered at the burning bush, could not and would not be outfought by Pharaoh and his troops.

In fact, Moses had got it wrong in one vital respect. They were not to 'stand still' but—in contradiction of all logic—to move forward, into the lake ahead of them. Moses was to lift up his staff, stretch out his hand over the water and divide it, so that the people could cross on dry ground. As he did what he was told, watched by the people in the fading light of the evening, two things happened. The column of cloud moved from the front of the camp to the rear, between them and the Egyptians, who were presumably settling down in their camp for the night. And a strong wind began to blow up from the east, which could be the 'human' explanation for the movement of the cloud to the west.

The pillar of cloud and fire is now described as 'the angel of the God' (v. 19), a description already familiar to those who knew the stories of their ancestors. Popular Christian tradition has dressed angels in shining robes and put wings on their backs, but the angels of the Bible are much less spectacular than that, for the most part. They came to share a meal with Abram and tell him of his wife's future pregnancy in old age (Genesis 18). An angel 'wrestled' with Jacob (Genesis 32). Gideon met the angel of God sitting under an oak tree at Ophrah, who accepted a sacrifice from him (Judges 6). In each case we are told that it was an angel and also 'the Lord'—in other words, in some way angels represent the presence and the purposes of God. Perhaps they were on these occasions human beings used by God as his messengers of comfort, vocation, or even warning. Many of us may similarly have experienced what we might call angelic ministry at moments of extreme need or emotion, in the guise of people—a nurse, doctor or special friend perhaps—who has brought into our situation nothing less than the presence of God for us.

Here we are left in no doubt that a heavenly intervention is involved. The cloud and fire were for the Israelites the promised presence of God. He was with them, and they only had to look up and see the sky lit at night, or the path marked for them by day, to know how real that presence was. In Christian terms, perhaps we could think of the cloud and fire as sacraments—'outward and visible signs of an inward and spiritual grace', as the old Catechism put it. The last thing one ought to do with a sacrament is to try to analyse it!

No doubt, despite their outwardly desperate plight, the Hebrews slept more soundly that night. Sheltering in their tents, they must have been aware of the howling wind ripping across their camp, but perhaps few of them realized to what extent it was to be the instrument of their escape.

The morning light revealed a remarkable sight. The wind had driven the waters back during the night, and there ahead of them was ground firm enough to walk across. At a signal from Moses, and led by the pillar of cloud which had now moved ahead of them again, they gathered up their things, loaded their hand-carts, and set off towards the other side.

What followed can be viewed, like many stories in the Hebrew scriptures, from two perspectives. To human eyes, what happened was that the Israelites, mostly on foot or accompanied by their domestic animals and perhaps small carts, made their way fairly easily across the bed of the lake. As they got to the other side the strong east wind, which had been holding back the water—presumably because the point where they crossed was relatively high ground compared to the rest of the sea bed—relented and the water began to seep back.

At the same time the Egyptians entered the lake. They were not on foot, however, but in very heavy chariots, pulled by heavy horses. Presumably the soldiers were also wearing armour of some kind. The wheels of the chariots sank into the soft bed of the lake and stuck. They couldn't move forwards or back. While they were attempting to get out of this predicament, a worse one befell them, as the waters returned and swamped them. The chronicler records with some glee that 'the entire army of Pharaoh' perished (v. 28). That is probably, in strictly historical terms, an exaggeration. At any rate, no such calamity is mentioned in Egyptian records. Nor did a Pharaoh die in such circumstances, although the Bible hints that the king perished too, without specifically saying so.

That would be a journalist's account of what took place, but we are also offered a divine perspective on these events. As we would expect, given the Hebrew view of happenings in God's world, every detail is masterminded by the Lord. He was the strategist; Moses carried out his orders. He sent the wind to blow back the waters, and he clogged the wheels of the Egyptian chariots. At God's command, when all the Israelites were safely across, Moses raised his staff and 'the sea returned to its normal depth' (v. 27), trapping God's enemies.

'Thus the Lord saved Israel that day from the Egyptians' (v. 30). All the others involved were obedient servants of his will, onlookers, or victims. It is the Lord's world and he alone controls it. The Israelites were the Lord's people, and he alone had delivered them.

In fact, both accounts tell the truth. One tells us what happened, but as usual the more revealing one tells us how and why it happened. All that happens in the created world is under the rule of its Creator. 'The earth is the Lord's and all that is in it' (Psalm 24:1). Pharaoh had defied the will of an almighty God, and his army, men, horses and chariots had paid the price for it.

As the Israelites gathered on the far side of the water, and especially as they saw by morning light that the Egyptian army had been simply swept away, one can only wonder how they felt. They were free at last, there was no doubt of that. After generations living in Egypt, including the more recent time of slavery, they had left that land for ever.

Goshen had had its compensations. There were houses, work and food. The soil was quite fertile. Even under slavery, there was a certain security. What lay ahead? So far as human eye could see, desert and scrubland, hot and unwelcoming. True, there was the promise of a distant land 'flowing with milk and honey', but it lay far away beyond many hostile tribes and many daunting physical obstacles. Freedom is a wonderful thing, but so is security and familiarity.

At this point they must, all of them, have been conscious that something greater than themselves was at work in their destiny. Over the centuries in Egypt they had clung to the faith of their fathers—faith in a single, almighty, infinite God. Now they had seen their God in action, tearing them free from the chains of slavery. The new challenge that lay ahead for them was to learn to trust him in less dramatic but equally testing situations.

A reflection

That is a scenario familiar to people of faith everywhere. To believe in an almighty God is one thing. To live by that faith is another. To embark on the journey of faith is to commit oneself to walk boldly into the unknown, secure only in the faith that the one who called you travels with you. That is the challenge to every Christian, just as it was to the motley crowd on the far side of the Sea of Reeds long ago.

THE PLACE OF HEALING

EXODUS 15:19–27

The Lord said, 'If you will listen carefully to the voice of the Lord your God, and do what is right in his sight, and give heed to his commandments and keep all his statutes, I will not bring upon you any of the diseases that I brought upon the Egyptians; for I am the Lord who heals you' (v. 26).

So the long journey begins. Euphoria, not surprisingly, marks its first few days, with the women, led by Aaron's sister Miriam (described by the writer as a 'prophet', we may note), joining in a triumphal dance accompanied by tambourines. 'Sing to the Lord, for he has triumphed gloriously!' (15:21). To escape from slavery, whether physical, spiritual or emotional, is indeed a wonderful thing, but as they were to learn, it was not escape straight into the promised land. What lay ahead was a desert. They had emerged from the nightmare of oppression into the more subtle but possibly just as demoralizing environment of the wilderness, a place where all the familiar landmarks of life had been erased and where they felt exposed and vulnerable.

This is a common experience for anyone emerging from an un-satisfactory or negative period of life. Most Christians who have come to faith through a moment of conversion will recognize the situation. There is euphoria at first, of course, but quickly they realize that they are not yet in 'paradise'. A long journey lies ahead, a journey which Jesus described as 'hard', on a 'narrow' and difficult road (Matthew 7:14).

The Israelites were embarked on such a journey. They had seen the power of God in delivering them from Egypt. Now they had to learn to trust him, and his servant Moses, on a long and arduous journey. As they left Egypt, we are told, 'the people feared the Lord and believed in... his servant Moses' (14:31). Now that belief would be put to the test, over months and years in an alien environment, with the constant threat of hostile tribes, hunger and thirst.

In the event, what happened to the Israelites was that when they faced difficulties—hunger, opposition, a bitter spring or an unvaried diet—they were quick to complain, apparently forgetting how God had always met their needs as and when they trusted him. It is easy to condemn these 'pilgrims through a barren land', but most of us would have to confess that the same springs of resentment, disappointment and selective memory are never far below the surface of our own lives, too. Having been promised freedom and a journey to a land 'flowing with milk and honey', the Israelites had missed Moses' honest explanation that this would take them through lands already occupied by warlike tribes, and the obvious fact that to cross several hundred miles of desert as a vast wandering column of men, women and children was always going to be a difficult and dangerous thing to do. A cycle of doubt, trust and renewal began which was to be repeated throughout their journey.

This is the picture of the classic journey of faith. It begins with the joy of release from the old life and the exciting possibilities of the new one, but we are deceiving ourselves if we think that the journey itself will be easy. Of course, as the Israelites found, there are moments of encouragement and security, oases in the desert, bread from the hand of God, victories over various enemies. The journey of faith, however, is usually a long one, and it is so in order that our faith in God should be tested and tried. The apostle Peter put it like this to Christians who had just faced the first wave of persecution at the hands of the Romans: 'You rejoice, even if now for a while you have had to suffer various trials, so that the genuineness of your faith... may be found to result in praise and glory and honour when Jesus Christ is revealed' (1 Peter 1:6–7).

So it is sad, but not surprising, that the people of Israel from time to time fell into this cycle of 'murmuring' and even rebellion against Moses' leadership, to be replaced by relief and even repentance when they discovered once again that God was with them, and that while he was, they were safe and on the right road.

Here, we read of the first of these 'murmurings', that kind of barely suppressed dissent that often dogs church life. They had trekked for three days in the wilderness of Shur without finding water. When they saw an oasis ahead, their spirits must have lifted, only to be dashed when they found that the water in the spring was bitter and undrinkable. They 'complained' to Moses, who in turn 'cried out to the Lord' (v. 25). God's answer to his cry was to direct him to a piece of wood (or possibly a whole tree) which was lying near the spring. He threw it into the water, and when the people tried it they found that it had become sweet.

Some experts on the area say that such a procedure is still sometimes carried out by nomadic tribes using desert oases. The wood of a particular aromatic tree can take away, or at least counter, the bitterness of the natural water, which was not of itself poisonous.

Whatever the scientific explanation, if any, the people were, of course, satisfied. Moses took the opportunity to remind them that the promise of God was to care for them on the condition that they did what was right and kept his commands. If they did that, then the Lord would be their healer.

Fresh from that experience of faith tested, they came to an altogether more congenial oasis, at a place called Elim, which means 'evergreen oaks'. Here were springs and palm trees, and the people presumably camped there contentedly. The numbers are, as usual in the Hebrew scriptures, highly significant. There were twelve springs (one for each tribe, as it were) and 70 palm trees, one for each of the elders of the people. The meaning isn't difficult to deduce: this was, at last, a stopping place prepared specifically for them, a true haven in the wilderness. It was a sign of God's care of them—provided they learnt to trust him.

A reflection

All spiritual journeys have highs and lows. We speak of 'mountain-top' experiences, but we know that there are also troughs as well as peaks— Bunyan's Pilgrim was on a journey to the Heavenly City, but he still had to cope with the Slough of Despond! Often a moment of great and thrilling revelation is followed by a chastening experience that brings us crashing down to earth. It happened to Jesus' disciples, Peter, James and John, when they came down from the mount of transfiguration, where they had momentarily glimpsed the kingdom of heaven, to be immediately confronted with an epileptic boy and his distressed father (Mark 9:2–19).

Such contrasts seem to be part of human experience. Perhaps the crucial thing is that we learn both from the highs and from the lows—something that the wandering Israelites seem to have found very difficult.

The Christian life is sometimes presented to seekers as a simple path to glory, but generations of disciples know that it is rather more than that. When Jesus said that 'those who endure to the end will be saved' (Matthew 24:13) he was speaking the unvarnished truth. But he promised to be with his people all the way and in every circumstance, 'to the end of the age' (Matthew 28:20).

FOOD FROM HEAVEN

EXODUS 16:1–16

'I have heard the complaining of the Israelites; say to them, "At twilight you shall eat meat, and in the morning you shall have your fill of bread; then you shall know that I am the Lord your God"' (v. 12).

The Israelites moved on into the wilderness of Sin. (There's no deep significance in the name, beyond the fact that Mount Sinai was to be found in it.) It was now ten or eleven weeks into their journey and probably the first excitement of the dash for liberty was wearing off.

The episode at Marah was now several weeks behind them. On that occasion their complaints had been met by God but accompanied by a warning that his willingness to defend and care for them was dependent on an attitude of total trust and obedience on their part. Typically, just those few weeks were long enough for the lesson to have been forgotten.

Probably, the full realization of what they had taken on in this desert exodus was just beginning to dawn. At any rate, the sight of the dry and hostile scrubland ahead of them seems to have provoked a fresh rash of complaints. Food supplies were getting low and it was obvious that there were few sources of replenishment ahead. Morale hit rock bottom, and the moans, when they came, were of a fundamental nature. Indeed, they questioned the value of the whole exercise.

'Why,' the people demanded of Moses, 'have you brought us into this wilderness to die? It would have been better if we had died along with the Egyptians—at least as slaves we had plenty to eat in Egypt!' (v. 3). So they argued, waxing lyrical about the brimming 'fleshpots' and being able to eat their fill of bread—forgetting, of course, the grinding labour and the whips of the taskmasters. How quickly memory can change the scenery!

These complaints were not from a small minority, either. According to the chronicler, 'the whole congregation' joined in (v. 2), besieging Moses and Aaron with their grievances. Promises of God's care for them, even the evidence of it in events they had seen with their own eyes, were not enough to silence them. In a mental situation that any human being can recognize, past experience was simply overwhelmed by present circumstances. They took their complaints to Moses, of course, but as he twice said to them—once in his own words, once in Aaron's—in fact, their complaints were not against him but against the Lord. It was God who had masterminded their release from Egypt. It was he who had shepherded them through the waters of the sea. It was he who guided them by day and night in the pillars of cloud and fire, and it was he who had provided the remedy for the bitter waters of Marah. Their sin was of unbelief, no less.

This much was powerfully put to the people, but in the positive context of God's promised action to meet their needs. He would, he told Moses, 'rain bread from heaven' on them, but even that gift would be a test of their faith and obedience, 'whether they will follow my instruction or not' (v. 4). And the instructions themselves were strange ones, involving the 'gathering' of food each morning, with a double portion to gather on Fridays in order to provide for the sabbath, when they would gather nothing.

The people were gathered for Aaron to address them, and as he spoke 'the glory of the Lord appeared in the cloud' (v. 10). Obviously this was a visible sign of some kind, perhaps a dramatic complex of sun and cloud in the sky. Whatever its form, it spoke to the crowd of God's presence, which is often associated with 'cloud' in biblical imagery. What Aaron said, in other words, God said—and they had better take note.

It was the proverbial mixture of good news and bad news. The bad news was that God had heard their complaining. They could no longer claim that they had simply raised the matter with Moses! The good news was that they would eat meat at twilight that evening, and their fill of bread in the morning. By that 'you shall know that I am the Lord your God'. It sounded wonderful, but unlikely. Where would 'meat' come from, or 'bread', for that matter? That was to be the test of faith. And when it came, as Moses would later explain, there would be strict regulations about how it was to be handled and shared out. That was to be the test of obedience.

So through a gift of grace—for that is what it was—God would teach his people a lesson in trust and obedience. It's a million miles from threats and punishment, and a million times more effective, as we shall see.

Of course it happened, exactly as Moses and Aaron had said it would. In the evening a large flock of quail alighted on the oasis, to be seized by the hungry people for their supper. Fresh meat—quite a luxury in the middle of a desert! Then, having filled themselves with meat before taking to their beds, they awoke in the morning to find the ground covered with dew, which, when it lifted with the rising sun, revealed a layer of something that looked at first like frost, though they knew it couldn't be that. Examining it, they found that it was a fine, flaky substance—white, rather like coriander seed and with the taste of wafers made with honey. After a splendid supper, this would make an equally delicious breakfast.

The people looked at it and predictably asked, 'What is it?'—a question which became its name. 'Manna' is more or less the Hebrew equivalent of 'Wotsit' (as in 'Wotsit's at the door'), a corruption of the question 'What is it?' Interestingly, that question remained unanswered, and despite many learned attempts to identify the substance by botanists, explorers and theologians, it still is.

The story of the manna has a far greater significance, however, than arguing about what it was! A fundamental truth of faith was at stake. It is God who supplies the food for the journey of faith. It's a point that Jesus made forcefully after he had fed the crowd with bread and fish. 'Very truly, I tell you, it was not Moses who gave you the bread from heaven, but it is my Father who gives you the true bread from heaven' (John 6:32). He went on to identify that 'true bread' as himself: 'I am the bread of life' (6:35). This life-giving bread was in contrast to the manna in the wilderness: 'Your ancestors ate the manna in the wilderness, and they died. This is the bread that comes down from heaven and gives life to the world' (John 6:49–50). Manna, in other words, fed the body and enabled it to survive. But the new 'bread' of which Jesus was speaking would do more than that: it would feed its eaters for eternal life.

These sayings of Jesus emphasize how central to Jewish understanding of their history was the story of the manna, the food by which God kept their forefathers alive on their desert journey. But it also shows how the concept of food for the journey lies at the heart of any notion of spiritual journeying. After all, in Egypt food was left in the tombs to nourish the dead on their journey into the dark kingdom of Osiris. How much more blessed was the food God provided to help his people on their long journey to the promised land—and how much more precious even than that is the spiritual food that God now provides for the pilgrims on the New Way, the way through Jesus to eternal life.

A reflection

Many of us will be aware in our own experience of this food for the journey—the 'viaticum' of Catholic piety. When we needed it most, God fed us. Our 'manna' may have been literally the Eucharist, signs and symbols of the grace by which he sustains us, but it may also have been another's prayer, or a friendly visit, or a word of scripture that spoke precisely to our need. Like the manna in the desert, it was not to be kept and hoarded: it was food for that day, and that day alone. Food is given to be gratefully consumed, to become part of us. As the modern health slogan says, 'You are what you eat'.

The manna helped to shape the people of the old covenant. Without

God, they would have perished in the desert. But so would we! In a very real sense, it is the 'food' with which God nourishes us that makes us what we are. Without God, the journey itself is simply not possible.

PUTTING GOD
TO THE TEST

EXODUS 17:1–7

He called the place Massah and Meribah, because the Israelites quarrelled and tested the Lord, saying 'Is the Lord among us or not?' (v. 7)

One might have thought that after the crossing of the sea and the miraculous provision of manna—both preceded by Israelite 'murmurings'—all such dissension in the camp would have been silenced. But human beings have very short memories, especially when they are faced with a present danger. Now it was not escape from the Egyptian army, or hunger, but thirst.

Water was always going to be a problem on this desert journey. Indeed, many experts have claimed that it was simply not physically possible for a crowd of many thousands of people to trek across Sinai. Such meagre supply of water as there was, in wadis and oases, would barely have been enough for the animals, let alone the humans. Yet the story stands. Even allowing for some statistical inflation by the chronicler of the numbers involved, a large tribe, formerly dwelling as slaves in Egypt, made their way to Canaan and eventually conquered it. To doubt that they crossed the desert is to doubt not a detail but the whole story of the Exodus.

The journey was not without its privations, of course, and here one of them is recorded—the availability of water. Between one oasis and the next, the people became aware that supplies were dangerously low. There were babies and children to be considered, as well as the elderly and infirm. They needed liquid intake to counter the desert heat and the demands of the journey itself. Suddenly, with the skin water bottles on their shoulders near to drying up, a moment of despair took command.

The complaints were the usual ones, presumably familiar enough to Moses and Aaron by now. 'Why did you bring us out of Egypt, to kill us and our children and livestock with thirst?' (v. 3). Once again the land of Goshen under Pharaoh seemed a better proposition than the wilderness of Sin under Moses.

This was no trifling spat, either. Moses said that the people were 'almost ready to stone him' (v. 4), which shows how desperate they had become. In other words, it was akin to rebellion against his leadership. This would have been bad enough if it were only a case of rejecting a once-respected leader who was now deemed superfluous to requirements, but for the Israelites, whose sole liberator and benefactor was God himself, it was tantamount to apostasy. As the Lord himself expressed it to Moses, they were casting doubt on his trustworthiness, rather than that of Moses: 'Is the Lord among us or not?' (v. 7).

God's response was surprisingly generous, given their repeated offence of 'quarrelling and murmuring'. Moses was given detailed instructions about his course of action. He was to take his rod—the one with which he had parted the waters of the sea—and go to a rock at Horeb. He was to strike the rock with his rod, and water would gush out of it. In that way, yet again, the people would see that God himself was with them as their source of strength and supply, and that Moses was truly his appointed leader. He had brought them out of Egypt across the waters of the Sea of Reeds; he had given them meat and bread to eat. Now he would give them water in abundance. Would they then finally accept that the Lord was among them?

Moses did as he was instructed, and the water gushed out from the rock. The people surged forward with pots, jugs and water bottles to fill them, and brought their animals to drink as well. I imagine they thought, 'Ah well, all's well that ends well!' Perhaps so, but their joy may have been somewhat tempered by the names that Moses gave to the place before they moved on—Massah and Meribah. They mean respectively 'test' and 'quarrel', and they were to be names engraved into the history of the people of Israel.

Centuries later the psalmist would warn the people of his day not to 'harden their hearts' as their ancestors did at 'Meribah and on the day at Massah in the wilderness', when they 'tested' the Lord 'and put me to the proof, though they had seen my work'. The people of that later generation were reminded of God's judgment on their ancestors in the desert: 'For forty years I loathed that generation and said, "They shall not enter into my rest"' (Psalm 95:8–11).

The Israelites sinned in 'putting God to the test', asking him for 'proof', doubting the reality of his promises, as so many people of faith have done ever since. If he provided water, then all was well. If on the other hand he failed to do so, they would have deduced from that that God had abandoned them.

'Is God really with us, or not?' That was what they were asking, but it was a question that God had already answered, many times over. They had the visible sign of his presence with them, in the pillar of fire and cloud. They had received the evidences of his care in the quails and manna with which they had filled their hungry stomachs. So why (it makes Moses' frustration with them understandable) did they continue to raise these doubts and demand further proof?

Fortunately, God's patience was not exhausted, though this incident was to be added to the long catalogue of their murmurings and complaints. He met their request. He vindicated his appointed leader, Moses. The water from the rock quenched their thirst and met their immediate needs, but this ugly incident permanently imperilled their share in the ultimate goal of their pilgrimage. They weren't to know it yet, but the generation who threatened to stone God's servant at Meribah would never set foot in the promised land—and neither would he. They had tried to put God to the test, but actually he was testing them, and they failed the test.

At the start of his ministry, Jesus went into the wilderness to be 'tested'—indeed, Mark's Gospel says that the Holy Spirit 'drove' him there (1:12). The testing took various forms, but one was to do something spectacular, like throwing himself from a pinnacle of the temple, to prove that he was indeed the Lord's Messiah. The reply of Jesus was based on this very story from the wilderness. The tempter was rejected with these words: 'Do not put the Lord your God to the test' (Deuteronomy 6:16). That is how Matthew records it, stopping short of the next words, 'as you tested him at Massah'. This one apparently insignificant incident became in Jewish thought the direst of warnings: you may ask, you may plead, but 'you shall not put the Lord your God to the test'.

A reflection

There is a huge lesson to learn here, but one that it is sometimes difficult to accept. Like Philip, we are sometimes tempted to say 'Just show us the Father and we shall be satisfied' (John 14:8), or, like Thomas, to demand a sign to confirm our failing faith. God does indeed give such signs, as many Christians, including myself, can testify, but not in response to demands. The Israelites had to learn to believe that what God promised, he would do. He would not have let them die of thirst in the wilderness. After all, he had brought them there!

We live in an age that fuels such demands. We want proof, evidence, confirmation that what we put our trust in is reliable. It is an absolute cornerstone of Christian faith—as it should have been for Israel in the wilderness—that God keeps faith, that he is 'faithful', utterly reliable in fulfilling what he has promised. In other words, as Thomas himself was told by Jesus, the answer to doubt is not evidence, but faith (see John 20:29).

THE LORD MY BANNER

EXODUS 17:8–16

Moses built an altar and called it, 'The Lord is my banner' (v. 15).

But when the fullness of time had come, God sent his Son, born of a woman, born under the law... so that we might receive adoption as children (Galatians 4:4–5).

Advent is seen by Christians as a time of preparation, and traditionally that preparation has included a constant reminder of the promise of Jesus to 'come again'. Now, Advent ends and we celebrate the fulfilment of an earlier promise, which was that God would in the fullness of time send the Messiah. It is, after all, the first coming that makes a 'second' coming possible! *Is. 9: 6*

The message from this is essentially the same as the one that the Israelites in the wilderness needed to learn—that God keeps his promises. As they left Egypt, he told them through Moses that he would be with them and would eventually bring them to the land of promise. Despite all their doubts and murmurings, in the end he did exactly what he had promised. On the journey he promised them both protection and provision. Again, he did exactly what he had promised, but the people found it hard to believe, especially when faced with hardship or, as in this episode, a powerful enemy blocking their path.

It was, in fact, inevitable that the incursion of a large tribe like the

Hebrews would evoke the suspicion of the tribes who already dwelt in the area. Resources were scarce and life hard enough without the arrival of thousands more mouths to feed. As Israel moved out of the deep desert into the more populated, though still largely barren, regions to the east of the Red Sea, hostility was likely from one source or another.

It came first from the Amalekites, a tribe associated with the Edomites, who were destined to become long-term enemies of the Israelites. As the Hebrew column wound its laborious way through the difficult terrain, the Amalekites prepared to attack. The caravan of people, animals and carts must have made an easy target, and although undoubtedly Moses had posted look-outs and there would have been armed men escorting the procession, they were something of a sitting duck for expert desert raiders like the Amalekites.

Probably the Israelites had seen their scouts and observed clouds of dust where horses and men were taking up position to challenge their advance. They could hardly have expected to make such a journey unopposed. Moses instructed his young general, Joshua, to get together an army and go out to fight the Amalekites. This is actually the first mention of Joshua, but he was, of course, destined to have a very significant role in the conquest of Canaan and the settlement of the Israelites there. While the armies took up position, Moses, Aaron and another elder, Hur, climbed to the top of a hill overlooking the action.

As battle was joined, Moses raised his hands in a sign of blessing, and while he did so Israel had the better of the battle. But when fatigue set in and he had to lower his hands, the Amalekites took courage and reversed the situation. Moses' colleagues got a rock for him to sit on and then supported his arms, one on either side of him, so that he could continue to bless Joshua's troops. Thus inspired, the Hebrews won the day and soundly defeated the men of Amalek.

God told Moses to see that a written record was made of the day's events and of the hostility of Amalek, as a judgment on the first tribe to oppose his people on their journey to the promised land. Moses did more: he erected an altar—probably a cairn of stones—and gave it a name, 'The Lord is my banner'. Like the regimental flag in the days of formal battles, the Lord was the 'banner' to which the people would look for inspiration. If this seems odd to the modern reader, then we might bear in mind the words of the national anthem of the United States, 'The Star Spangled Banner', which is all about precisely such a moment of inspiration drawn from the sight of the Stars and Stripes in the midst of battle. God—not the hands of Moses, in some supposed act of magic—was to be their inspiration, the one to whom they looked in moments of desperate need. They should rally around him, like troops around the flag, and even lay their hands on the flag to dedicate themselves to his service. That, at least, is one possible interpretation of the rather baffling saying, 'A hand upon the banner of the Lord'.

What is quite clear is that we are not dealing here with some magical power in Moses' hands, or in the staff that he carried with him. The fact that the fight went well when his hands were raised in prayer, and went against God's people when his hands fell, is not to imply that Moses had the power to influence the outcome of the battle. That power was only and entirely the Lord's. What varied with the sight of Moses at prayer was the people's trust in the Lord. His figure on the hill with uplifted hands was a kind of sign of God's blessing upon the army of Israel. When they looked up and saw their leader doing what God commanded, they rallied. When they saw him falter, their faith in God was weakened. It may seem rather immature to depend in such a way on a human sign, but at that moment it was as far as the people's faith had come. All through the journey their faith was inconsistent and greatly influenced by circumstances. It needed constant bolstering. Moses standing there on the hill during the battle, like the Lord's flag or banner flying bravely in the heart of the conflict, was a reminder of God's presence with his people.

One conclusion that the chronicler drew from this story was that by their attack on the Israelites the fate of the tribe of Amalek was sealed: 'The Lord will have war with Amalek from generation to generation' (v. 16). In human terms, this was but one manifestation of the tribal wars which constantly afflicted people living in such deprived areas. But in divine perspective, Amalek was seeking to prevent God's great purpose—one which would eventually bring blessing not just to Israel but to the whole world. To oppose the divine will is the deadliest of sins, and over the centuries it would seem that succeeding generations of Amalekites were to suffer its consequences.

A reflection

This story is not so much one of supernatural intervention, much less of some mysterious 'power' inherent in Moses' rod or even his blessing, but of reliance on God. The people had to learn to trust him, however dark the prospect seemed to be.

Advent, which ends tonight as we begin to celebrate the first coming of Jesus, in his birth at Bethlehem, is a season of hope based entirely on the faithfulness of God. Again, however dark the prospect (and at times it will be very dark), we are called to trust his faithfulness. 'In the fullness of time' he sent his Son (Galatians 4:4), but the people had become restless at the delay. In the fullness of time, he has told us, the same Lord Jesus will come again, but often our hearts, too, are restless at the delay. 'Where is the promise of his coming? ... All things continue as they were from the beginning of creation' (2 Peter 3:4).

Bethlehem should remind us that God keeps his word. Tonight, as we recall the glorious fulfilment of one promise in a birth at Bethlehem, may it strengthen our hearts to believe that in every respect God is faithful.

WHAT'S IN A NAME?

EXODUS 18:1–4; MATTHEW 1:21–23

'You are to name him Jesus (Yeshua), for he will save his people from their sins' (Matthew 1:21).

The name of the one was Gershom... and the name of the other, Eliezer' (Exodus 18:3–4).

All through the Bible, names are important, probably more important or significant than names are to people today. In biblical times, your name was your character as well as your identity, telling the world what your parents hoped of you. And in the process of life, those names would change (which leads to some confusion for modern readers at times) to reflect changes in the person's status, responsibility or qualities. So Abram becomes Abraham when God makes him the father of a mighty family to come (Genesis 17:5). 'Abram' means something like 'exalted ancestor' and 'Abraham' the 'ancestor of a mighty tribe'.

It's often instructive to look at biblical names as evidence not of identity, but of character and qualities. We may be sure that godly parents chose their children's names carefully (as one hopes they still do!) and that subsequent renaming offers an insight into the significance of what happened to them later in their lives. I suppose the equivalent would be the 'baptismal name' that Christians are often given if they are baptized late in life, especially when the person comes from a non-Christian culture or religion.

We may assume that when Moses' Midianite wife Zipporah bore him two sons, he named them thoughtfully. The eldest he called 'Gershom', because he himself was then 'an alien in a foreign land' (*ger* is the Hebrew word for 'alien', as mentioned earlier). Perhaps the name was to express gratitude to the Midianite people who had welcomed him and from whom he had taken a wife and now had a son. Perhaps, too, there was a hint of regret in it, for Moses' own people, the Hebrews, had been aliens for hundreds of years in Egypt, and were at that moment a long way from finding a homeland where they would be citizens.

The second boy was named 'Eliezer', which means 'God my help'—*Eli* (God) and *ezer* (help). The explanation of the name given here is that 'the God of my father was my help, and delivered me from the sword of Pharaoh' (Exodus 18:4), although in fact Eliezer was born before Moses set off back to Egypt to confront the king and demand the release of his people. Presumably, therefore, the name originally spoke of a prayer or a faithful hope that God would be his helper, and the events that transpired gave the name a greater significance. As the young man stood in front of Moses in the moment of reunion (at which we shall look more closely in the next chapter), such a thought must have been in the father's mind. His faith had sometimes wavered or at least been sorely tested, but the Lord had indeed been his helper. But for that help, the people would not now be here, within journeying distance of the land of promise.

On this particular day of the year—Christmas Day, if you are reading the book faithfully through from Advent—names are also significant. In Joseph's dream of the angel, he was told that his wife Mary would bear a son who had been conceived 'from the Holy Spirit', but he was also told what the child was to be named: 'Jesus, for he will save his people from their sins'. The name, as it were, would determine the divine purpose behind this miraculous birth. The child's name, Jesus—Yeshua in Hebrew, which is in fact also rendered as 'Joshua'—was that of a mighty Saviour. The connection with this wilderness story is in that detail, for here a greater Joshua was being born, who would also lead his people across the waters into a new and promised kingdom. But this time the waters were to be the waters of death, and the promised land was nothing less than the kingdom of heaven.

There is another name in Matthew's narrative—'Emmanuel' (1:23). This was the name that the 'virgin' would give to her son, as prophesied by Isaiah (7:14). In fact, Jesus was, so far as we know, never actually called 'Emmanuel' by anybody, but the title retained its significance—'God with us'. At Bethlehem, in some mysterious way, the God of eternity entered the world of mortality in the person of this infant. 'The Word became flesh and dwelt among us' (John 1:14). And then, right at the end of Matthew's Gospel, we have the promise that although in physical presence Jesus was to leave the earthly world, he would be 'God with us' to the end of human time (Matthew 28:20).

Names matter, especially biblical ones. In many ways, the name tells us all we need to know to understand the purpose of the coming of Jesus and the deep meaning of his life. 'He will save his people from their sins', and 'he will be with us, even to the end of the age'.

A reflection

As Moses' little family from his desert days—father-in-law, wife and two sons—met him at Rephidim, we can sense again the strength of human ties that bind a family together. At the call of God Moses had left them, but in thought and prayer these God-fearing desert folk had not forgotten him.

We think today of the 'Holy Family', cast in our minds in a little tableau of the stable, the manger and the animals. But at its centre lay a baby who had also left his Father in heaven to fulfil his purposes on earth. Ahead lay years of preparation, of ministry, of teaching and miracles and lives transformed, and at the end a cross of wood and then a borrowed tomb. But also ahead lay the fulfilment of that purpose, the 'crossing of Jordan' and the opening gates of the kingdom of heaven.

SHARING THE BURDEN

EXODUS 18:5–27; ACTS 6:1–8

'They will bear the burden with you. If you do this, and God so commands you, then you will be able to endure, and all these people will go to their home in peace' (Exodus 18:22–23).

'Select from among yourselves seven men of good standing, full of the Spirit and of wisdom, whom we may appoint to this task, while we, for our part, will devote ourselves to prayer and to serving the word' (Acts 6:3–4).

It's rather fitting that this story, of Moses sharing his administrative burden with the elders, should be our reading for St Stephen's Day, or 'Boxing Day', as it is usually called in Britain, when we recall how the apostles also came to share their workload with the seven 'deacons', among them a man called Stephen. An interesting difference is that Moses was persuaded to this move by his father-in-law, while the apostles seem to have arrived at the same conclusion collectively, but on their own!

As we have just noted, names in the Bible tend to change, or sometimes they got rendered differently in different languages. Sometimes, perhaps, scribes misrecorded them. The father-in-law of Moses first appears as Reuel (Exodus 2:18) but becomes Jethro in the next chapter (3:1) and always subsequently. Just to add more confusion, he is called Hobab in Numbers (10:29) and Judges (4:11)!

Whatever his name (and Jethro seems much the most likely), he seems to have been an extraordinary man, well able to cope with being father-in-law to the equally extraordinary Moses. He was a Midianite, and at any rate at this stage in the story is a leader among his people, as a chieftain or priest. When Moses returned to Egypt at God's command, Jethro took Moses' wife Zipporah, and the two small sons, back to the tribal home. But clearly there was no antagonism involved, and having heard that his son-in-law had succeeded in leading the Hebrews out of captivity in Egypt he made his way towards Sinai and found Moses and the people camped at 'the mountain of God' (Exodus 24:13). He had brought Zipporah and the two boys, Gershom and Eliezer, with him to meet Moses, and one must assume there was an emotional reunion.

It is touching that Moses went out to meet Jethro and bowed down to him, before kissing him and inviting him into his tent. There the full story of the escape from Egypt was told, firmly set, of course, in the initiative and action of the Lord. The pagan priest seems to have had no problem with this. Indeed, rather more: he 'rejoiced for all the good that the Lord had done to Israel' (Exodus 18:9). It is noteworthy that he spoke of 'the Lord'—Yahweh, that is. Indeed, he went on to speak a blessing from the Lord and to acknowledge that he is 'greater than all gods, because he delivered the people from the Egyptians' (v. 11). He then provided a sacrifice and burnt offering to God and formally broke bread 'before the Lord' with Aaron and all the elders of Israel. It is a remarkable example of uncovenanted grace—of God welcoming a sincere God-fearer even though he was outside the community of the covenant. It is, perhaps, a warning not to draw our lines of religious exclusion too tightly.

Moses invited Jethro to sit in on a public 'judgment session' the next day, when those people who had grievances or complaints could bring them to Moses. Not surprisingly, the session lasted all day. When it was finally over, Jethro took Moses aside and remonstrated with him. What was he doing, taking all this upon himself? Moses' reply was simple—because the people came to him as God's agent of law, and he could make known to them the provisions and instructions of God.

Jethro was not deterred. 'What you are doing is not good. All you will do is wear yourself out. Why not seek out and appoint some assistants, men of wisdom and judgment, who will be able to deal at least with the simpler cases? They can always refer difficulties to you.' Moses could see the force of his argument, and did what his father-in-law had proposed, thus establishing a judicial system that lasted hundreds of years, into the time of the kings of Israel.

There are two issues here which are relevant to all of us on our pilgrimage of faith. One is practical, and the other theological.

Practically, the story is about recognizing when things have got beyond us and being prepared to accept help. Moses was an exceptionally gifted and charismatic leader. That is obvious from his achievements. He was also a man of great personal courage and faith. Yet it needed a voice from the past, a father-in-law from a desert tribe, to point out what one might have thought he would see for himself —that he could not take to himself alone the burden of judging the people.

Why had he not seen it? Was it that he had become isolated in his role, lacking in trust of his colleagues? Was it a form of pride—the 'it's all right, I can cope' syndrome? Was it perhaps that he felt God had called him to this task and it was his sole responsibility? Could it even have been that his faith itself was the 'problem': to share the task would in some way imply a lack of trust in the Lord to meet all his needs?

We are not called to judge Israel! But the attitude of mind that is reluctant to call for help, or to accept it, is familiar enough, and those who have gone through a time of grieving, for instance, will know how hard it sometimes is to admit that it's all got beyond us and we need help. We may even feel that our faith in God should be enough, without human help. Yet isn't it true that it is through human help that God usually touches our lives? By rejecting it, we may be rejecting the ministry of angels.

The theological aspect is the value (not just the practical

effectiveness) of shared responsibility. The picture of leadership in the early Church is entirely of a shared, collaborative ministry, from the time when Jesus sent out his disciples in pairs to the apostolic practice of appointing a plural leadership in the new churches (see, for example, Titus 1:5 and James 5:14). There can be no doubt that when Moses took Jethro's advice the whole procedure of judging the people improved. More people were involved; there was more opportunity for difficult cases to be discussed by the elders and Moses; and a greater sum total of wisdom was applied.

The principle behind all of this was not 'democracy', though obviously this new arrangement spread authority more widely than before. It was based on what is called 'theocracy', the rule of God himself. In principle, God alone was the ruler of Israel. He could delegate that authority, as he had done to Moses; and in turn Moses could delegate it to others, in this case the elders. Later, that authority was to be delegated to the judges and eventually the kings, but the authority itself was always God's. As the psalmist sang, 'Rise up, O God, judge the earth, for all the nations belong to you!' (Psalm 82:8). That principle lies behind all understanding of authority in the Bible, both Old and New Testament. The 'throne' on which God is seen to sit is the throne of judgment, and from him all justice and all mercy ultimately flow.

A reflection

Christians are told to 'carry one another's burdens' (Galatians 6:2), but no one can share our burden if we insist on carrying it ourselves. A lesson learnt from a father-in-law in the desert may well speak to burdened hearts and lives 3,000 years later. The story of Jethro's advice for Moses, and the leader's decision to heed it and share the burden of responsibility, provides a link with the story of Stephen, the man whom we commemorate today as the first Christian martyr. It is a moving contrast to remember him on the day following our celebration of the birth of Jesus and a reminder that there is more to Christmas than carols and mince pies!

In the early days of the Church, the apostles were similarly over-whelmed with practical responsibilities. 'It is not right that we should neglect the word of God in order to wait on tables,' they said (Acts 6:2). One of those who was chosen for this apparently menial, or at any rate purely organizational, task was Stephen, 'a man full of faith and the Holy Spirit' (6:5).

Of course, Stephen didn't confine himself to waiting at tables or organizing rotas, or we shouldn't be remembering him today. His courage in preaching the gospel, and even confronting the Jewish Sanhedrin, didn't depend on his organizational skills, but much more on his faith and on the Holy Spirit. In him, we have the model of those who are called 'from the ranks', as it were—just as Moses' helpers were—to serve the Lord, and then find themselves in the forefront of the action.

KINGS AND PRIESTS

EXODUS 19:1–9

'You have seen what I did to the Egyptians, and how I bore you on eagles' wings and brought you to myself. Now therefore, if you obey my voice and keep my covenant, you shall be my treasured possession out of all the peoples. Indeed, the whole earth is mine, but you shall be for me a priestly kingdom and a holy nation' (vv. 4–6).

The Israelites moved on from Rephidim into the desert of Sinai. This was far from being the most direct route to Canaan, but there was a divine purpose in the detour. It took them to the foot of Mount Sinai.

There had already been three awesome events in the story of the people's liberation—the burning bush, the Passover and crossing the Reed Sea. Now a fourth was to be added, which would also have a major role in the formation of the emerging nation's identity and character. Indeed, perhaps this was even more fundamental than the others, for at Sinai the Law of God was to be 'handed over' to Israel—the Law which was to mark them out for ever among the nations; the 'divine difference', as it were, between them and those around them. After that, one more of these foundational events was to take place—crossing the Jordan river. The picture of the new nation would then be complete in terms of its distinguishing beliefs, culture and history. The wandering tribe of Hebrews would truly be a nation.

But for now there was the matter of the Law. Clearly the people already recognized the rule of God, because Moses taught them God's commands and instructions and they had seen both the blessings and the penalties that could follow from keeping or breaking them. Now something more was promised. The Lord himself would 'appear' on Sinai to establish and confirm the covenant agreement that bound this people to him for ever.

A covenant, in biblical terms, is a promise which requires a response. Here, for instance, the Lord's message to Israel through Moses is that they will be his 'treasured possession' if they 'obey my voice and keep my covenant'. The promise is a clear one, but it expects, and is even made conditional upon, a specific response.

There had already been two covenants offered by God in the story of the Bible up to this point. There was his covenant with the human race after the flood, when God promised never again to destroy the earth and designated the rainbow as a 'sign' of the promise (Genesis 9:9–11). That seems to have been an unconditional covenant. After that, there was God's covenant with Abraham, following the testing of his faith over the sacrifice of Isaac (Genesis 22:15–18). This was a promise that Abraham's descendants would have a land of their own and be God's special people. It would seem that the third covenant, at Sinai, is a renewal of the second, but with more detail—particularly in spelling out what would be required of this 'special people'.

'I bore you on eagles' wings and brought you to myself' (v. 4): the picture is a beautiful one, depicting the exodus as a soaring flight to freedom. As the people nursed their blistered feet they might have wondered what had happened to the 'eagles' wings', but they must also have been aware, even in their worst moments, that their release from Egypt was entirely God's doing. The only blow struck in the whole exploit was the one with which Moses felled an Egyptian taskmaster, and that was long before he was called at the burning bush.

It was God who had brought them out—but he had brought them 'to himself'. That's an interesting phrase, with its implication that although they were for ever free from slavery to the Egyptians, they had now entered into a new relationship of dependence. They were to be God's, to belong only to him. They would be his 'possession', albeit a 'treasured' one. Out of the riches of the whole earth, which is his, he would meet their needs, but they would be for him a 'priestly kingdom and a holy nation' (v. 6). That was the nature of the covenant.

That phrase sets out a huge responsibility for this emerging people. What was a 'priestly kingdom'? They knew what a priest was, and they knew what a king was. A priest was a person who represented God to the people and the people to God, and a king was a person who exercised rule and authority. What may have given them pause was the idea that there could be a 'priestly kingdom'— a society where God's rule and authority were represented to the nations and through whom those nations could come to God. It was obvious that such a people would need to be a 'holy nation'—a people 'sanctified', set apart, consecrated for this special role. It may all have sounded more than a little daunting, a terrifying mixture of responsibility and privilege.

If that was how it felt, then it was no less than the sober truth, and over the generations the Israelites would discover that to be 'chosen' by God is much more of a responsibility than a privilege. From now on they would be judged by higher standards than the neighbouring tribes. From the foot of Sinai would emerge a people set apart—consecrated—for God. As they quickly found out, however, it is not only gifts that are consecrated at the altar. So are sacrifices. 'You only have I known of all the families of the earth; therefore I will punish you for all your iniquities' (Amos 3:2). From now on the journey would not be easier, but harder—a journey towards God, a journey of progressive consecration. The direction would be right, but the going (in every sense of the word) would be tough. Perhaps that is the mark of every journey towards the 'promised land'.

A reflection

In his first epistle, addressed to Christians dispersed across the Middle East, the apostle Peter describes them in similar language to these words in Exodus. They are 'chosen', 'sanctified' (1:2); they are a 'chosen race, a royal priesthood, a holy nation, God's own people' (2:9). The language of the Old Covenant is applied to the people of the New.

As for the Israelites of old, the privilege carries the responsibility and the burden. The path to God is strewn with obstacles. To be called to be sanctified is not yet the same thing as actually being sanctified! Most of us are aware that it can be a difficult and painful process at times, as it was for the people of Israel.

But then, whoever said it would be easy? Certainly not Jesus: 'the gate is narrow and the road is hard that leads to life' (Matthew 7:14). But neither we, nor they of old, travel alone, and the destination is infinitely worth it.

THE HOLY MOUNTAIN

EXODUS 19:9B–35

As the blast of the trumpet grew louder and louder, Moses would speak and God would answer him in thunder (v. 19).

Here, in the most vivid and colourful language imaginable, is the story of the fourth great event in the emerging history of a new nation, the giving of the Law. As if to emphasize that this was to be no rule of human devising, its conveyance to Moses and Aaron and thence to the people is marked by all the symbols of divine presence. As the people waited at the foot of Sinai, their clothes freshly washed, their bodies ritually consecrated to God (which meant that sexual intercourse was forbidden), the mountain itself, which was to be the setting for the revelation, was racked with what might in natural terms be described as a volcanic eruption. A thick cloud enveloped the peak and smoke rose through it while the whole mountain shook violently.

Moses had warned the people to prepare themselves, and they had done so for three days. Strict limits were set around Sinai and dire penalties were threatened on anyone—man, woman, beast, or even member of the priestly tribe—who crossed them. It was meant to be terrifying, and a vivid picture of its impact on the collective Jewish memory is preserved in the New Testament, in these words from the letter to the Hebrews: 'You have not come to something that can be touched, a blazing fire, and darkness, and gloom, and a tempest, and the sound of a trumpet, and a voice whose words made the hearers beg that not another word be spoken to them. (For they could not endure the order that was given, "If even an animal touches the mountain, it shall be stoned to death". Indeed, so terrifying was the sight that Moses said, "I tremble with fear")' (Hebrews 12:18–21).

Moses had told them that the Lord would 'come down' upon Mount Sinai 'in the sight of all the people' (v. 11), but what that meant in fact was that they would be able to see and hear the signs of his appearing without, of course, actually seeing God himself. Even Moses was not to have that privilege, though later in his life he begged a sight of the glory of the God in whose Name he had acted for so long and in such difficult circumstances. God granted him a moment of revelation—a vision of his glory, seen from the cleft of a rock where Moses was hidden. But he was only to see 'the back' of God, not his face: 'for no one shall see my face and live' (see Exodus 33:17–23). It is a unique moment in the Hebrew scriptures, in one sense almost naïve in its conception of the nature of God, yet in another sense profound beyond description. We may 'see God's glory', and by his mercy and grace we sometimes do, but on earth we cannot see his 'face' (the full revelation of who he is). Of course, for Christians there is the belief that we have 'seen the Father' in his Son (John 1:18; 14:9), but the fullness of that revelation waits for the day when we shall see him 'face to face' (1 Corinthians 13:12). All of this, of course, is the language of mystery.

So is the account of the giving of the Law on Sinai. There were blasts on a trumpet 'so loud that all the people in the camp trembled' (v. 16). As the mountain loomed over them, full of sounds and fire and smoke, Moses and Aaron took their leave of the people, and—hearts doubtless thumping—made their way across the limits and upwards towards the summit.

If the divine object was to emphasize to the watching people that something awesome, dreadful and terrifyingly significant was about to take place, it was effective for a time. But, as we shall see, such is the frailty of human nature and the brevity of its memory that even under the shadow of all this they began to have doubts.

The next twelve chapters of Exodus leave the story of the pilgrimage and set out the provisions of what came to be called the 'Mosaic Law'. Even a cursory reading will reveal that it covers moral laws, social regulations and ritual instructions. Most people are aware that the 'ten commandments' were received by Moses on Sinai, and indeed they are there at the head of the list, great and eternal moral truths that many nations have made the basis of law and ethics. It is not hard to believe that they came as a revelation of God to Moses, in whatever way that revelation took place. We shall consider them in the next chapter.

The remaining rules and regulations are obviously in a different category. We shall be looking at them in a later section of this book. It is hard to see their precise connection with the moral and social laws, but it is not difficult to believe that during their quite lengthy stay on the mountain Moses and his brother were able to organize and codify the various sacrifices and offerings of the people, some already widely in use. In the atmosphere of that sacred mountain, it would be foolish to describe the fruit of their labour as 'man-made'. For them, and eventually for the people too, all of this—moral, social and ritual—taken together made up 'the Law', the way in which their communal and religious life was to be led from that day on. It was the defining identification of the people God had 'called' to be his own.

A reflection

'The presence of God' is a difficult experience to describe, yet on the journey of faith most pilgrims are at times aware—sometimes in a powerful and insistent way—that God is 'near' to them. For myself, the experience of bereavement, miserable and painful as it often was, became at times transformed by an overwhelming sense that God was with me. Others have testified to exactly the same experience, one well expressed in the words of

the psalmist: 'Though I walk through the valley of the shadow of death…
you are with me; your rod and your staff—they comfort me' (Psalm 23:4).
God does not, it seems, spare us times of sorrow and loss, but he does
promise to accompany us through them.

In contrast to the gentle promise of the Divine Shepherd, we have the
revelation of his presence here at Sinai. There is probably no story in the
whole of the Old Testament that makes the presence of God as dramatic
and evident as this one. The people had already trekked an enormous
distance—at least 200 miles—across desert terrain and the rocky foothills
of the mountain range. Much of their initial enthusiasm for the journey had
waned. It was to this people, in their time of doubt and anxiety, that God
chose to stage (I can't think of a better word) his most dramatic and visible
revelation. Smoke, fire and trumpets set the scene. Thunder was the voice
of God to the people. Surely now they would believe that God was with
them, whatever their outward circumstances?

THE LAW OF GOD

EXODUS 20:1–26

I am the Lord your God, who brought you out of the land of Egypt, out of the house of slavery; you shall have no other gods before me (v. 2).

There were many codes of law among the various civilizations of the ancient world, and some of them have survived to take their place in libraries around the world. But it is safe to say that none achieves the sheer grandeur of thought and universality of application of the Decalogue, the 'Ten Commandments'. Apart from the commandment about the Sabbath, all of them express profound moral or religious truth, and indeed the law of the Sabbath, which guarantees to the people a day of rest each week, might be considered a fundamental human right.

The commandments are introduced not with any royal or governmental authority but with the divine imprimatur. These are the laws of God. They begin with the majestic words of our 'key verse': 'I am the Lord your God' and a reminder that his authority over them flowed not from conquest or election but from his acts of salvation. 'I am the Lord your God who brought you out from the house of slavery'—therefore 'you shall have no other gods before (in the sense of 'beside') me'. They were his people, because he had set them free in order to bring them to himself (19:4), and because they were his 'treasured possession' (19:5) he was now to give them the keys to a truly human life, life as God planned for it to be lived.

In one sense, these are the 'maker's instructions' for human life. Followed, life would be effective, happy and satisfying. Ignored or disregarded, life would fall to pieces. Like a neglected car or lawnmower, with the maker's handbook lost long ago, it can't be expected to work properly.

The commandments start with human beings and God, not surprisingly. Morality, in the ultimate sense, always depends upon the basic loyalties of the individual person. If one's loyalty is to self, or to a group or nation, that will determine the individual's behaviour. These laws are based on the premise that there is no higher loyalty than to God, and that if a person gets that loyalty right then right behaviour should flow from it. Hence idolatry, which is at heart placing any object or person before God in our loyalty, is a fundamental sin.

To speak of God as 'jealous' (v. 5) seems strange, because jealousy, in the normal use of the word, is a most unpleasant and destructive fault. However, God's 'jealousy' could more properly be called 'possessiveness' (again, not usually an attractive trait), in the sense that these were his people, his 'treasured possession', and he could not bear to see them tempted away from his 'steadfast love'. The notion of punishing children for the sins of their parents is, again, an unattractive one, yet it is an observable fact that parental faults are often the cause of their children's distorted or unhappy lives. These words are words of warning. It is not, perhaps, the place of a code of law to offer remedies for those who fail. We would have to look forward to the vision of a loving God offered by the later Hebrew prophets, especially Isaiah, and of course to the teaching of Jesus, to see how divine mercy can also break the bonds of this heritage of family failure.

The commandment about the 'misuse' of the divine name falls in the same category (v. 7). It is about reverence for God. After all, it is one thing to believe in him (in the sense of an affirmation that he exists, or is even all-powerful). It is a step further to regard with reverence the God we say we believe in. This speaks of a proper sense of awe in our approach to God—a sense, perhaps, sometimes endangered by the almost matey familiarity that pervades some modern worship.

Of course it goes further than that. If we 'take the name of God', as the Israelites did, and as Christians do, then we bear a solemn responsibility to reflect that 'taking of his name' in the kind of life we live. To call ourselves 'Christian' and act in an unChristlike way is, as I see it, flagrantly to break this commandment. It is certainly much more (though not less) than a simple matter of using the name of God or Jesus as a swear word.

The commandment about the Sabbath (vv. 8–11) goes into more detail than the other Ten Commandments, almost seeming to shift over into the category of the ritual laws that follow. The principle is clearly enunciated first: 'six days you shall labour and do all your work. But the seventh day is a Sabbath to the Lord your God' and on it 'you shall not do any work'. Which particular day of the week is observed seems to be a secondary matter. The primary concern is that human beings, and human society (which is a different matter), should recognize the need for a 'fallow' day, free from the burdens and demands of daily work. There are no rules as to how that day is to be observed, beyond the prohibition of work of any kind—and not only for the head of the family, but for all its members, its servants, its guests and even its animals! It's hard to match this commandment with the modern Western Sunday, with shops and supermarkets busy and tens of thousands of people hard at work enabling the rest of us to have our 'day of rest'.

The command to honour parents (v. 12) is, as the Bible points out, the only commandment which includes a promise or reward. Those who respect and care for their parents will themselves live long and rewarding lives. The neglect of the elderly by their own families is one of the besetting moral and social failures of our society. A local councillor in Oxford told of a man who phoned to enquire how he could go about registering a complaint with the social welfare department (and presumably seeking compensation) after his elderly father was found dead in a flat, where his body had been undiscovered for fourteen days. The son was quite shocked when the councillor suggested that the neglect was the family's every bit as much as the council's.

The remaining commandments cover what are generally recognized as fundamental offences against morality—murder, adultery, theft and lying testimony (vv. 13–16). The final commandment, to avoid 'covetousness' (v. 17), is interesting, in that it looks at a primary cause of offence rather than the offence itself. To desire what belongs to another could well be the root of many a murder, theft or act of adultery. There is merit in addressing the cause rather than seeking to punish the action itself, and in very down-to-earth language this commandment sets out to do that.

The people were fearful at the phenomena that accompanied the giving of the Law, and expressed their fear to Moses. His words are a beautiful commentary on these commandments, and indeed express very well the whole Jewish attitude to the Law of God. It is not a burden, but a gift. 'God has come only to test you and to put the fear of him upon you so that you do not sin' (v. 20). The Law, in other words, was to guide a people who 'feared' (in the sense of 'revered') God into a safe path away from sin. It was then, and it is now.

A reflection

British drivers are familiar with the 'Highway Code', which is intended to be a manual of safe travel on the roads. While most of us don't, I suppose, constantly refer to it, or decide to stop at red traffic lights because we are 'commanded' to do so, we recognize that our own safety and that of other road users does in fact depend on it. Every journey needs its 'rules of conduct'.

That is also true of the pilgrimage of faith: it is a journey to freedom, but it is a journey within disciplines. The lesson that the Israelites were so slow to learn is one that many a traveller along the road of faith has also struggled with. God's will for us is our total freedom to be everything that he has created us to be, but we shall never arrive there until we have learnt to travel under his direction. For Israel, the 'Highway Code' was the moral and religious law of Sinai. If they lived by that, their journey would be a successful one. If they ignored it or, worse, disobeyed it, then the journey would hit insuperable roadblocks.

For us, the 'Highway Code' of the new covenant is different. It has few religious laws, few compulsory rituals or ceremonies. It does involve, however, a total faith in the Father and the Son and a complete openness to the Spirit. 'If the Son makes you free, you will be free indeed' (John 8:36): free to follow Christ, free to do the Father's will, free to hear the prompting and wisdom of the Holy Spirit. There is simply no such thing as an undisciplined, indulgent, please-yourself kind of Christian discipleship. He calls; we follow. He guides; we are led.

REGULATIONS
AND RULES

EXODUS 21:1—23:19

You shall not follow a majority in wrongdoing; when you bear witness in a lawsuit, you shall not side with the majority so as to pervert justice; nor shall you be partial to the poor in a lawsuit... You shall not oppress a resident alien; you know the heart of an alien, for you were aliens in the land of Egypt (23:2–3, 9).

These chapters contain an amazing mixture of laws, some magisterial in their lofty justice—to aliens, to creditors, to the poor—some dealing with what one might see as the trivia of rural life, including such matters as compensation for animals injured when for hire or killed by falling into an uncovered pit. Many carry the death penalty, often for offences that may seem to us relatively unimportant, such as failing to control an ox that had a tendency to gore. With the best will in the world, it seems difficult to think that all of these, and many more rules about ritual and worship in the tabernacle, were dictated in precisely this form to Moses and Aaron, still less carved on stone tablets. Two hundred men—let alone two—would have been required to carry them down the mountain.

More probably, as is suggested by a closer reading of them, these laws may be taken as amplifications relating to particular cases of the general ethical principles set down in the Ten Commandments.

Probably some were the product of what we might call 'case law', as the principles of the Decalogue were applied to actual cases that came before the elders or the priests. Some were intended to reflect the character of God, and some the concern for others that lies behind many of the moral commandments.

What they do raise in a powerful way is the issue of justice. A tribe wandering across the wilderness would eventually become a nation in a settled land. Such a people needed a system of law, one that related to their own particular situation as a 'theocracy', a society seeking to live under the direct rule of God. Law of this kind tends to evolve, but at its best it evolves according to consistent principles. Reverence for God, care for the elderly, honesty in social and business life and a spirit of contentment would make for such an evolution, and they are the very heart of the Ten Commandments.

Jesus summarized these principles under two categories. We are to love God with heart, mind, soul and strength. And we are to love our neighbour as ourself. 'On these two commandments,' he said, 'hang all the law and the prophets' (Matthew 22:40).

In contrast to the universal truth of the Ten Commandments, it would be unwise to try to apply these rules and regulations to the details of modern life and society. Not many of us are in a position to pawn our neighbour's cloak (22:26), but if we did it is to be hoped that we would not simply let him freeze during a cold night for the lack of it. The aforementioned goring ox would incur different penalties for its wilfully negligent owner according to whether it had killed an adult (21:29) or a male or female slave (21:32). In the former case the penalty was death and in the latter only a fine of thirty shekels of silver.

At the same time, we do have a doctrine of manslaughter, which is applied to those who cause loss of life by wilful negligence, precisely the principle involved here. And all of us have a duty of care for those who, through our own actions, may be impoverished—and the return of a cloak may not always meet the needs of the case!

Underlying these laws is a wonderful concern for justice and mercy. Twice, the Israelites are told to remember that they were once aliens and therefore should never oppress aliens in their own land (22:21; 23:9). (Clearly this refers to a time after the desert wanderings when presumably resident aliens were rather scarce in their ranks.) They are also told not to 'pervert justice due to the poor' (23:6), and in apparently minor details there is a touching concern to create a genuinely caring and forgiving society: 'When you come upon your enemy's ox or donkey going astray, you shall bring it back' (23:4). It is hard to legislate for kindness, of course, but these laws certainly recommend a way of life that recognizes the rights of others.

Alongside this care for others, however, there is (to the modern reader) a remarkable lack of concern for slaves. If a slave-owner should strike a slave—male or female—with a stick, injuring them so badly that they die, he will be 'punished' (in an unspecified way). This was, in fact, a vast improvement on the accepted practice of the time, which recognized no fault in such an event. On the other hand, should the slave manage to survive for 24 hours, 'there is no punishment, for the slave is the owner's property' (21:21). This seems a strange attitude on the part of a people who were themselves for long years slaves in Egypt. How quickly we all forget!

Some of the commandments given here are about festivals and ritual obligations, although these are dealt with more fully in Exodus 25—31. They are presumably placed here in the Sinai section of the narrative to imbue them with the full weight of divine authority. They cover, in enormous detail, the building of the tabernacle and the ark, including their decoration, and the choosing and anointing of the priests, the 'sons of Aaron'. There are regulations about offerings and sacrifices and a fascinating account of the choosing of gifted craftsmen and artists to make the coverings, carvings, vestments and utensils of the tabernacle (31:1–11).

While all of this is not really part of the wilderness story, it is a fascinating glimpse into the kind of society and culture that was being forged there, a culture which had at its very heart the deep conviction that moral choices were not simply a matter of individual taste or preference, but of that 'virtue' which mirrors the character of

God himself. That seems to be a truth we neglect at our peril. After all, while it is true that these rules and regulations are mostly 'local' to the people of Israel at that time and in that social setting, they are based on principles of far greater moment. Behind them lies a system of ethics based on respect for God and his creation which has down the ages revolutionized human thought and often brought great blessing to people and nations.

A reflection

It sounds like a preacher's cliché to say that the moral law of God is much like the Highway Code (as I suggested earlier), and of course it is unlike it in one important way: it carries the ultimate in sanctions—eternal judgment. But in other respects it matches the Code exactly. God's law exists because of need, not whim; it deals with real, not theoretical, problems; it is respected and widely observed (because it tackles those problems); and it brings good to those who keep it, and avoids the damaging effect of the evils that it sets out to counter.

God gave the Law for human good, not because he wished to exercise arbitrary authority over his creatures, and he left us free to disobey or disregard it (though at our peril). However, in a strange way it is the Law itself, not the disobeying of it, that sets us free—free to be all that God has intended for us. As with Israel, so with us: he sets us free in order to bring us to himself.

Like the skilled pianist or ballerina, within the freely accepted discipline there is, of course, restraint, but there is also the greatest freedom of all— the freedom of fulfilment. As the psalmist said, 'I find my delight in your commandments, because I love them' (Psalm 119:47).

NO COMPROMISE

EXODUS 23:20–33

'I am going to send an angel in front of you, to guard you on the way and to bring you to the place that I have prepared. Be attentive to him and listen to his voice; do not rebel against him, for he will not pardon your transgression; for my name is in him. But if you listen attentively to his voice and do all that I say, then I will be an enemy to your enemies and a foe to your foes' (vv. 20–22).

It is hard to piece together any kind of orderly sequence to the events surrounding the giving of the Law. Taken literally, it would seem that Moses and Aaron, and sometimes the elders, were constantly running up and down the mountain, passing on snippets to the people and returning to the clouded top for more. For all sorts of reasons this seems unlikely. Perhaps it is best to see the whole narrative as one event, looked at from different angles—Moses', the people's, even the Lord's—with the actual sequence of secondary importance.

For instance, this powerful exhortation, introduced with a promise of angelic help, comes in the middle of a quite bewildering array of rules and regulations about all kinds of things, from culinary practice ('you shall not boil a kid in its mother's milk', 23:19) to farming methods ('the seventh year you shall let the land rest and lie fallow, so that the poor of your people and the wild animals may eat', 23:11).

Then suddenly the tone changes. The people are on their journey to the promised land once again. An angel—a messenger of the presence of God, no less—will lead them and instruct them. 'My name is in him,' says the Lord—that is to say, he bears my authority in full. So they must 'listen attentively' and do what the angel says. If they do, their enemies will become God's enemies and the way ahead will be clear.

A stern note of warning about compromise follows. As they move into the lands of the Canaanite tribes, the Israelites might be tempted to begin to worship their gods or follow their religious practices. But that way disaster lies, for they will share the fate of the other tribes, who will be ravaged with pestilence. Instead of copying their practices, they are to make no compromise with them. Their altars and pillars are to be demolished, and the Israelites are to worship only 'the Lord your God'. In that way, they would be blessed with food, water and health.

There is also included a warning about the timing of all this. The tribes won't be driven out instantly: 'little by little I will drive them out from before you, until you have increased and possess the land' (v. 30). To speed up the process would be disastrous, because until the numbers of the Israelites had grown they would not be numerous enough to ensure that the land wouldn't become desolate or be taken over by wild animals.

It sounds like a well-devised military strategy, and it is tempting to imagine Moses, Aaron, Joshua and the others drawing it up during the 40 days that we are told they were up Mount Sinai. What was more important, of course, was that they, and eventually the people, should recognize it as more than simply a man-made plan, but part of a divine purpose. Only that sense of vocation would ensure that this slow migration of former slaves would eventually lead to the creation of a new nation 'under God'. That was the divine vision for them, forged on the slopes of Sinai and overshadowed by the hovering presence of Yahweh. It was to be sealed, as it were, in the renewing of the covenant between God and his people (Exodus 24:3–8), after which the leaders gathered on the mountain were offered a vision of the glory of the Lord. Their destiny from now on would be as a people called, set apart—not for their own blessing, but (as God told Abraham long ago) so that 'all the nations of the earth shall be blessed' (Genesis 22:18).

However we choose to read the story of the wilderness journey, it is impossible to remove from it the sense of the presence of God with his people without taking the very heart out of the narrative. In some way, and with at times highly unpromising material, God was working out a purpose that would ultimately bring blessing to the whole human race. It is a wonderful truth of faith to believe that he still is.

A reflection

The promise of an angelic presence with the Israelites, to guard them on the way and to bring them to the prepared place, raises the question of angels in the Old Testament. There are a number of stories of angels, from the angels who visited Abraham and Sarah in their tent to the angel who spoke with Gideon under the tree. There are also the angelic horsemen and chariots of fire that ringed the hillside when Elisha was threatened (2 Kings 6:17). On the other hand, several times the 'angel of the Lord' seems to be identified with the Lord God himself, as in this case. 'If you listen to his voice (that is, the angel's) and do all that I say (that is, God), then I will be an enemy to your enemies.' Not only that, but we are told that 'my name is in him (the angel)'.

All of this reinforces the impression that angels are those who fulfil God's commands and bring his presence into situations that he wishes to influence. Whether particular angels are human beings, called for a time to this special purpose, or spiritual beings of another order completely, or simply a kind of shorthand for 'the presence of God' is a question that may not be answered this side of heaven. People cannot 'see' God with human eyes but in these manifestations (whether human or superhuman) they can 'see' and 'hear' him.

In the New Testament, angels are also at work, of course. They are active in the events surrounding the birth of Jesus and at the resurrection. They are at work in the early days of the infant Church, as though the precious new 'baby' needed special care. But many of us would feel that we too, in our own time, have experienced the ministry of 'angels', often in the form of people who have come to us at moments of great need or distress as agents of God's strength, wisdom or love.

MOSES ON THE MOUNTAIN

EXODUS 24:1–18

Then Moses took the book of the covenant, and read it in the hearing of the people; and they said, 'All that the Lord has spoken we will do, and we will be obedient' (v. 7).

In the story of the long journey of the people of Israel, Sinai is much more than a detour en route. Indeed, in one sense it is the linchpin of the whole enterprise, for it was during this period and out of this experience that the nation and its religion were born. The 'book of the covenant' presumably included many of the rules and statutes that God had already revealed to Moses during that mountain-top encounter. But more importantly, it was the heart of a solemn agreement between the Lord, Yahweh, on the one hand and the 'people of the covenant' on the other. By keeping his laws they would mark themselves out as his people, and by guiding and protecting them he would define himself as their God. In line with the common practice of the time, such a solemn agreement was sealed with sacrificial blood, which was splashed over the people.

The 'words of the Lord' referred to here concern 'ordinances', and perhaps we can distinguish them from the moral law that was enshrined in the Decalogue, the Ten Commandments. These 'words' were apparently written down by Moses, whereas the commandments are described as engraved on tablets of stone by God himself (Exodus 32:16). The significance of this would be like the significance of a personal signature on a deed or cheque. These were the commandments of God and those who flouted them would be answerable to him. That is the point of the argument, and it is both unhelpful and unimaginative to waste time wondering how a God who is 'spirit', without 'body, parts or passions', could physically engrave a stone.

'Covenant' is one of the great words of the Bible, and certainly the Jews came to see themselves as 'the people of the covenant'. They would already have been familiar with the idea, because most of the ancient cultures had some form of 'covenant' between ruler and ruled, and in some cases between tribes. This kind of covenant set out the conditions, often in great detail, which must be kept to make it effective, along with whatever was offered by the ruler if it was fully kept. A few of these ancient tribal covenants still exist, usually in partial form, and one can see how similar in language and process they were to this covenant on Sinai. For instance, they were usually sealed with a sacrifice, often involving an animal being cut into sections, and often ended with a kind of 'promissory note': do this, and these are the good things that will flow from it.

The form of the covenant on Sinai has obvious similarities, but the 'stipulations', as we might call them, are vastly different. This is not a covenant between a ruler and a vassal people, but between a God of justice and holiness and a people whom he is calling to be his in a unique way. So the stipulations are about behaviour, justice, honesty, worship, sacrifices and devotion to God. The promises, with which we are now quite familiar, were of the protection and guidance of God on their journey to the land he had promised them and in the future.

Covenants of this kind are binding on both parties, provided the terms of the covenant are met. The Hebrew scriptures frequently refer to the Lord as a 'God who keeps covenant', or a 'God of faithfulness'. There was, in other words, no doubt to be cast on God's willingness to keep his 'side' of the agreement. The problem was always on the human side. Living by commandment is always difficult and sometimes irksome. As the Israelites encountered the practices of the tribes around them, they may sometimes have felt that here was a less restrictive lifestyle than theirs—no Sabbath, no constant requirement to offer tithes and sacrifices, no expectation of eternal devotion to a single deity. Perhaps pagan religion looked more 'fun': it was certainly a great deal more permissive. More probably, the Israelites were simply uncomfortable with the notion that they were fundamentally 'different' from the surrounding tribes. Although it is satisfying, at one level, to be 'special', there is a deep human antipathy to the notion of being odd or peculiar, and there was little doubt that the religion and lifestyle that the God of Israel required of them did look both odd and peculiar to the neighbouring peoples.

At any rate, and whatever the immediate causes, the history of the people of Israel from Sinai onwards is of a nation struggling to fulfil its side of the covenant. In the language of the prophets, they were a 'wayward' people, disobedient, stubborn, easily drawn away from the worship of the one true God. They were a covenant people, of that there was no doubt, but their side of the covenant was in constant jeopardy—and the pattern of disobedience was set early in its history, as we shall see.

For 40 days (a timespan which was to become significant in Jewish thought) Moses was alone on the mountain, having been called to ascend it after a six-day manifestation which was seen by all the people. The 'glory of the Lord settled on Mount Sinai', in appearance like 'a devouring fire on the top of the mountain' (v. 17). On the seventh day, the 'Sabbath' as it were, Moses was called to make his way alone up the hillside, entering the cloud that covered its slopes. Moses, Aaron, Nadab and Abihu, and 70 of the elders, had already been granted a vision on the hillside of the God of Israel, but whatever that vision was to them, it was clearly of a different order from the encounter Moses alone was about to have with the Lord. Its culmination comes in words of disarming simplicity: 'When God finished speaking with Moses on Mount Sinai, he gave him the two tablets of the covenant, tablets of stone, written with the finger of God' (Exodus 31:18).

At Sinai God gave the people of Israel two priceless gifts, the law and covenant. By those instruments he made them his own, distinct and separate from the nations and tribes around them, and called them to be agents of his purpose and mission in history. Over the centuries, this privilege was often to seem an unbearable burden. They didn't want to be 'different', separate, holy, and there were times when they longed to be released from what they sometimes found to be irksome restrictions. Yet only in following the divine purpose could there be blessing—for themselves and, ultimately, for the whole human race.

Like the Israelites of old, Christians are familiar with the feeling of being odd, distinctive, even peculiar in the eyes of their neighbours. There is an enormous invisible and perhaps unspoken pressure on them to conform to the standards and values of the society in which they live. The apostle Paul called on the Christians in Rome—the contemporary capital of the opposition worldview, we might think—not to be 'conformed to this world, but be transformed by the renewing of your minds' (Romans 12:2). J.B. Phillips paraphrases the same verse beautifully in his *Letters to Young Churches*: 'Don't let the world around you squeeze you into its own mould, but let God remould your minds from within.'

This is the perennial problem for the Christian pilgrim on the long journey from the birthplace of faith to the glory of the promised land. Bunyan wrote about it in *Pilgrim's Progress*: remember Vanity Fair? Imperceptibly at times, we may find that our 'true intent, to be a pilgrim' is being undermined by the insidious voice that says, 'There's no harm in it, everybody does it.'

These were the temptations that were to lie ahead for the Israelites, like traps and snares on the path. The difference for the Christian, of course, is that it is not a matter of obedience to a set of rules, rituals and regulations that marks us out, but the priority of kingdom values—those distinctive marks of the disciple of Jesus that are love, justice and mercy.

A reflection

God created months with the movement of the moon, and years with the passing of the seasons, but it is human beings who create calendars. We are creatures of time, and it's hard to miss in a story like that of the wilderness journey the chronicle of its passage. Centuries were spent in Egypt, several years on the journey to Sinai. There was the annual Passover to remind them where their emerging nation had come from, and worst of all there was the penalty of the 40 years which was to make the last part of the journey, from Sinai to Canaan, so protracted that none of the adults who set out on it would complete it. Yes, the Israelites would have been deeply conscious of the passing of time!

Today is New Year's Day. Here is our chronicle of passing time, offering us an annual opportunity to look back and assess where we have been and forward to what we may yet become. Above all, for the Christian, there is the belief, as Wordsworth put it, that 'Our times are in His hand, who said, "A whole I planned".' It is that 'whole life' of which we are stewards and for which we shall one day be called to account—a solemn thought!

THE GOLDEN CALF

EXODUS 32:1–18

When the people saw that Moses delayed to come down from the mountain, the people gathered around Aaron, and said to him, 'Come, make gods for us, who shall go before us; as for this Moses, the man who brought us up out of the land of Egypt, we do not know what has become of him' (v. 1).

If seven days is a long time in politics, what are forty for a people who have lost their leader in the desert? Moses had disappeared over a month ago up this forbidding mountain, with its thunder, lightning and cloud. Suddenly, the Hebrews were without their leader, the man who had interpreted the will of God to them and led them painstakingly along the path to freedom. Where was he? How could any man survive for forty days alone up a mountain in the desert? If he had not died of exposure, there were the perils of hunger, thirst and wild beasts. It's hardly surprising that something like panic swept the Israelite ranks.

They went to Aaron, the recognized spokesman and deputy of Moses. Deprived of their human leader and of the confidence in God that he had brought to them, they pleaded for 'gods'. As for Moses — 'this Moses', as they called him, 'the one who brought us up out of Egypt' (quite forgetting that it was the Lord, and the Lord alone, who had done it)—'we don't know what's become of him'. The tribes around them had gods who seemed to serve them well enough. The Israelites wanted at least to be on level terms.

So they argued. Forty days had been long enough to erase their memories of the triumphant release from Egypt, laden with gifts and led on their way by the angel of God in a pillar of cloud, and even their recent promises of lifelong devotion to the Lord and his commandments. They wanted 'gods'!

Aaron acceded to their demand. It's hard to work out why. Perhaps he was just slightly jealous of his brother and his greater standing with the people. Perhaps the crowd were in an ugly mood and he was simply afraid to deny them. Or perhaps—though this seems incredible of a man who only days before, according to the chronicler, had stood on the same mountain and seen 'the God of Israel', standing on 'a pavement of sapphire stone, like the very heaven for clearness' (24:10)—he too now had his doubts. At any rate, he gave in, and even organized the creation of a golden calf, cast in a mould from the earrings of the women, perhaps some of the rings given them by terrified Egyptian women on the night of their escape from slavery. As the golden calf—a young bull—came from the mould, the people shouted, 'These are your gods, O Israel, who brought you up out of the land of Egypt!' (v. 4).

The image of a golden bull-calf had many precedents in the religions of the region. The Egyptians had a bull-god, Apis, with which the people would have been familiar during the years of slavery. The Canaanite tribes used a bull image in the worship of the baals. It's interesting that, in making this image, the Israelites did not feel that they had rejected the Lord so much as 'reinterpreted' him. They thought that they could worship Yahweh through the bull image, in the same way as their neighbours worshipped their gods. Indeed, Aaron had an altar built in front of the image and proclaimed that the next day should be a feast day to the Lord.

And so it was. Sacrifices were offered, both burnt offerings and 'sacrifices of well-being' (v. 6). When the religious rites were complete, the people set to for a party, sitting down to eat and drink and then rising up to 'revel'. The word translated here as 'revel' is also used in the Old Testament with sexual connotations (for example, Genesis 26:8 and 39:14), and certainly in Canaanite culture such sacrificial feasts were often accompanied by sexual activity that was thought to promote fertility in the crops or the herds.

Meanwhile Moses, far from perishing on the mountain, is involved in what one can only describe as a prolonged spiritual encounter with God. In this process of revelation (for that is what it seems to have been) the Lord made him aware of the misdemeanour of the people. The chronicler sets it out in the language of a dialogue, which is a common device in the Hebrew scriptures to describe a process of growing understanding of the nature and character of Yahweh. We have already seen Abraham engaged in such a 'dialogue' (Genesis 18:22–33). Unless one is to understand that both Abraham and Moses were wiser and better beings than God, it can only be assumed that what these dramatic conversations describe is the process by which a human mind, tuned in to the will of God, comes to apprehend the mysterious processes of the divine mind.

In this case, God's fierce anger is the first part of that understanding. The people 'have acted perversely; they have been quick to turn aside from the way that I commanded them... I have seen this people, how stiff-necked they are.' This anger is then expressed in judgment: 'Now let me alone, so that my wrath may burn hot against them and I may consume them' (vv. 7–10).

The dialogue continues, switching between Moses and the Lord, with Moses 'reminding' God how he had brought the people out from Egypt with great power. Now, if the Israelites were to be consumed in the desert, wouldn't the Egyptians have cause to mock his purposes? Again, one assumes that this was part of the inner process by which Moses could work through his own anger and disappointment, slowly realizing that God had not brought the people this far in order to abandon them. After all, there was the covenant promise to Abraham and his descendants. How could that simply be set aside?

'And the Lord changed his mind'—literally, 'repented'—as though Moses was right and he was wrong! (v. 14). Yet surely what had happened in this traumatic spiritual experience was that Moses, in a heightened state of awareness of the presence of God, was able to understand both the mercy and the holiness of God. The Lord will not destroy what he has saved. It was not that God 'changed his mind', but that Moses came to a clearer revelation of the character of God, who could hate the evil the people had done while retaining his covenant love for them.

Moses then took the tablets of stone bearing the commandments of God, and began to make his way down the mountainside. At some point he was met by Joshua, who then accompanied him. As they reached the lower slopes, Joshua remarked on the noise he could hear from the camp below. He assumed the Israelites had been attacked; it sounded like the noise of battle. But Moses (who already knew, of course, that things had gone drastically wrong) corrected him: 'That's not the noise of battle that you hear, but the sound of revellers' (v. 18).

A reflection

On the journey, in moments of disappointment, fear or despair, we are prone to look for 'other gods'. In the modern world it may be alcohol or drugs, or a new relationship, or a bout of self-indulgence—buying a new car or expensive jewellery or clothes. Sometimes it may take a more overtly 'religious' form. Many bereaved people, I have discovered, turn, at least for a while, to the 'other gods' of spiritualism. Sport can become another 'god', and so can essentially good things like art, music or poetry, if we give them the place we once kept for God himself. The truth is, there are as many 'other gods' as there are people, and only an individual knows what is for them the 'golden calf' that supplants the true and living God.

It can also happen when the journey turns sour. Rather like the Hebrews, suddenly without their leader, we may find the spiritual pilgrimage suddenly a barren trek without a beloved pastor or teacher who has been our constant helper and example in the past. Or we may find that such a person, whom we trusted and depended on, has been revealed to have feet of clay. We feel cheated and let down. The temptation then is to cast around for another god, a substitute for the one we have lost—who was not, of course, God at all, but simply (like Moses) a messenger or channel of the grace and power of God for us.

It is hard when we already feel we have our backs to the wall, rather like the children of Israel in the wilderness, to be deprived of the very people we have relied on. But it is disastrous to think that we can 'create' substitutes for them. 'These are your gods, O Israel!'—what a pathetic cry it really was! There is only one God, and in the end our trust has to be in him rather than in his earthly ministers, however gifted, sincere and godly they may be. God knows our need, however, and time and again, experience tells us, it is in those moments of apparent helplessness that the prayer of the stricken heart goes right to the heart of God. It's as though he says, 'I am with you, in joy and sorrow, in laughter and pain, in success and disappointment. Look up, and see the pillar of cloud by day and the pillar of fire by night! I will never leave you comfortless.'

SIN AND JUDGMENT

EXODUS 32:19–35

'But now go, lead the people to the place about which I have spoken to you; see, my angel shall go in front of you. Nevertheless, when the day comes for punishment, I will punish them for their sin' (v. 34).

Moses carried the precious tablets carefully down the mountainside. In his arms, engraved in stone, was the first commandment: 'You shall have no other gods beside me.' Just below it was the second: 'You shall not make for yourself any idol... you shall not bow down to them or worship them.' Yet as he came near to the camp he saw that the people had already, and in the most flagrant way, broken both of them. The sight of the bull-calf and the celebrations was too much for him. In fury he threw the tablets of stone to the ground and broke them. The people had broken the commandments of God, even before he had delivered them. He broke the stones that bore the sacred words—what use were they now?

Then he seized the calf and ordered that it be melted down and ground to powder, which he mixed with water and ordered the Israelites to drink. He then turned his anger on Aaron. 'How could you let the people do such a thing? Why did you let them persuade you?' After all, Aaron, with the other leaders, had seen 'the glory of the Lord' on the mountain. How could this miserable model represent the Creator of all that exists?

Aaron's excuse was, by any standards, pathetic. First, he blamed the people ('you know what they're like!'). Then, by implication, he blamed Moses: they had asked for gods to lead them because Moses had disappeared away up the mountain for so long. Then he tried to imply that the fire was somehow at fault. True, he had asked them to hand over their gold ornaments, but when they threw them into the fire 'out came this calf'! In other words, it was either magic or divine. He wasn't to know which and surely could hardly be blamed for it. Needless to say, Moses was not impressed, especially when he saw that the people were 'running wild' with Aaron's permission —behaviour which would have been scorned even by the idol-worshipping tribes around them.

Moses, still hot with anger, then stood at the gate of the camp and called out, 'Who is on the Lord's side?' In response, the men of the priestly tribe, the Levites, ran and stood around him. He then took the most drastic punitive action, sending them through the camp on a mission of death, slaughtering on his instructions one brother, one friend and one neighbour each. When the gruesome task was done, Moses congratulated them, telling them that by their loyalty they had ordained themselves as a tribe for the service of the Lord (v. 29).

This violent action of Moses seems to have been an effective shock tactic. Undoubtedly the people were stunned by the ferocity of his reaction. Like many of us, they probably hadn't thought of a little bit of idolatry as all that serious, but now they could be in no doubt about the depth of disobedience that they had plumbed.

By the next day, Moses had calmed down a little. He told the people that although they had indeed committed a great sin, he would 'go up to the Lord' to see if he could, perhaps, make some atonement for their sin (v. 30).

When Moses turned to God in prayer, it was in fact to plead for forgiveness for the people. His language is moving, coming from the heart of a true mediator. If God was not able to forgive their sin, then would he please also blot Moses out of 'the book that you have written' (v. 32)—presumably, the book of the covenant. Moses identified so closely with the people, even in their sin, that he could not imagine himself saved while they were condemned.

The answer of the Lord was clear and categorical. 'Whoever has sinned against me I will blot out of my book' (v. 33). There could be no bargaining or compromise on the principle of divine justice. Yet that statement was followed by what amounted to a recommissioning of Moses. He was to go now and 'lead the people to the place about which I have spoken to you' (v. 34). There was, in other words, no 'Plan B'. 'Plan A' was still in place. The journey would continue and God through his angel would go in front of them. Not even human sin of the most destructive kind can deflect the purposes of God. In that respect, nothing had changed.

Yet one thing had changed. Although the angel of the Lord would go with them to lead them, there would be punishment for their sin. It came swiftly, there in the desert: 'The Lord sent a plague on the people, because they made the calf—the one that Aaron made' (v. 35). No magic, no hint of divine sleight of hand there. This was human sin, the product of human will and human disobedience— Aaron's, and the people's. It had already led to bloodshed, in the slaughter by the swords of the Levites. Now it was nature's turn, as a plague swept through the camp. Yet God was still, as Moses had come to appreciate, a God who hates sin but loves people. Even under judgment, they were still his 'precious possession'.

There is no such thing as a sin-free pilgrimage, not unless the pilgrims are all angels! But this story of the golden calf—so flagrant in its disobedience, so catastrophic in its consequences—can offer the Christian pilgrim both warnings and encouragement.

First of all, sin struck when the people were at a low ebb, physically, emotionally and spiritually. They had been camped in the wilderness of Sin a long while, instead of pursuing their journey to the promised land of milk and honey. There was precious little of either of those in the desert, of course. Footsore, often hungry, anxious about their vulnerability to hostile tribes and suddenly deprived of their charismatic leader, Moses, who had disappeared up the mountain for over five weeks, it's not surprising that they felt

helpless and abandoned. They had experienced the terrifying phenomena on the mountain—fire, thunder, lightning and what sounded
like trumpet blasts—but only at a distance, unlike the hand-picked
leaders. They had been kept back from seeing 'the glory of the Lord'.
It is at times like that, when we feel weak, helpless and alone, that
faith faces its most severe trials.

On the other hand, Christians may take comfort from the perspective that the gospel offers us on this story. 'The wages of sin is
death', as the people discovered to their dismay when Moses eventually
came down from Sinai and saw what had happened. But the apostle
Paul, quoting those very words, adds immediately, 'but the free gift of
God is eternal life through Christ Jesus our Lord' (Romans 6:23). There
is an answer to the defilement of sin which was not available under the
old covenant, because it is God's gift 'through Christ Jesus'.

But there is more. Moses offered himself as mediator on behalf
of the people, an offer that was rejected by God on the basis of the
immutability of his justice: 'Whoever has sinned against me I will blot
out of my book.' Moses could not really be a mediator between God
and the people because he was one of the people. You can't be a 'one-
sided' mediator. Now, however, there is such a mediator. 'There is one
God,' the same Paul writes; 'there is also one mediator between God
and humankind, Christ Jesus, himself human, who gave himself a
ransom for all' (1 Timothy 2:5–6). Here is the perfect mediator, the
divine Son of man, who is not only 'one of us' but one with the Father.

A reflection

*In an hour of weakness, forgetting too quickly the promises of the covenant
that they had so recently made, the people of that covenant sinned, and paid
the price in suffering, plague and death. It was horrible, but however one
looks at it the wounds were self-inflicted, and in mercy God still kept his part
of the agreement, sending his angel to lead them on their way to the place he
had chosen for them.*

In our hours of weakness, often forgetting equally quickly past mercies and blessings, we, the people of the new covenant, are also prone to sin. In mercy God provides a mediator and an advocate in his Son, promising forgiveness to those who repent and his continued presence on the journey to the place he has prepared for us. God is still the God who hates sin but loves people. That can be an important thought for the journey, especially when we are most conscious of weakness and failure.

LIVING FOR THE FUTURE

DEUTERONOMY 1:22–40

I said to you, 'Have no dread or fear of them. The Lord your God, who goes before you, is the one who will fight for you, just as he did for you in Egypt before your very eyes, and in the wilderness, where you saw how the Lord your God carried you, just as one carries a child, all the way that you travelled until you reached this place' (vv. 29–31).

Eventually the people of Israel were able to leave Sinai, doubtless chastened by their experience but also encouraged by the sight of the wagons bearing the material of the tabernacle, the 'tent of meeting' whose design, furnishing and ornaments had all been part of the long revelation of God's will on the mountain (Exodus 25—27). Before they left Sinai, Moses had anointed and consecrated it (Numbers 7:1–2). This was how God's people would worship him, as a pilgrim people, a people on the move, yet always with the Lord their God at the centre of their communal life. When they stopped, the tabernacle was erected, and when they moved on, it was taken down.

If they had gone straight from Egypt to Canaan, the journey would perhaps have taken them two years. As it was, those two years had already elapsed before they set off on what should have been the final stage, northwards from Sinai and eventually across the Jordan into Canaan. As we have seen, it had never been easy or straight-forward. The terrain was difficult and the challenge of the journey across desert and scrubland daunting even for a party of fit young men. To move a whole tribe, with old and young, with babies and the elderly and infirm, must have stretched faith and endurance to their limits. Needless to say, frictions and disagreements arose, and with depressing frequency the people, or a section of them, would question the validity of the whole exercise.

Perhaps more seriously, Aaron, no less, and his sister Miriam questioned Moses' right to regard himself as the sole mouthpiece of God's messages: 'Has the Lord spoken only through Moses?' they asked (Numbers 12:2). The immediate cause of their criticism was the fact that Moses had taken a Cushite wife. It seems that God was not opposed to this apparently strange decision. Instead, he punished Miriam, who became leprous—a condition that Moses pleaded with God to reverse. In fact, her 'sentence' was reduced to seven days as a leper. Not long after, though, she died. In all of this the Lord confirmed that he did indeed speak to his servant Moses, and only to Moses, 'face to face' (Numbers 12:8).

Yet on they went, notwithstanding setbacks and dissensions, the 'angel of God' before them, Moses, Aaron and their lieutenants bringing up the rear. The details of the journey onward from Sinai are recorded in a fragmentary kind of way in both Numbers and Deuteronomy, but the outline of the story is clear enough. They reached Kadesh-Barnea, which put them within reach of their eventual destination. Moses decided that the time had come to check out the land of Canaan, which God had promised would be theirs. Spies were selected, one from each of the twelve tribes, and told to go ahead and assess the prospects.

When the spies returned, there was a majority report and a minority one. Ten of the spies, while agreeing that the land was indeed fertile—'flowing with milk and honey' (Numbers 13:27)—nevertheless felt that it would be foolish to try to conquer it. The people were strong, the towns fortified and (a nice touch for a nervous audience) the men were so large that they made the Hebrews look like grasshoppers. This report terrified the crowd, who began to recite their usual complaint to Moses. 'Why did you bring us here to perish under enemy swords? It would be better for us to go back to Egypt'. Indeed, so serious were they that they proposed choosing a captain and making their way back to the land of their slavery (Numbers 14:3–4).

The other two spies, Caleb and Joshua, had a quite different view of things. They agreed that the land was fertile—everything that the Lord had promised them—but they were confident that the resident tribes could be conquered. 'If the Lord is pleased with us, he will bring us into this land and give it to us' (Numbers 14:8). Nevertheless the people were not persuaded. In fact, they threatened to stone Caleb and Joshua to death.

At this point the Lord intervened, appearing at the tent of meeting in his 'glory' and saying to Moses that he had now had his fill of the people's unbelief and disobedience. They would be struck with pestilence and disinherited. His promises would pass to another nation. Again Moses pleaded for God's mercy, and again God agreed to forgive them. But—and it was a huge 'but'—not one of the people presently over twenty years old would enter the promised land, apart from the families of the two faithful spies, Caleb and Joshua.

Later, as they made their way into the wilderness of Zin, there were further similar rebellions by the people, who never seemed to learn the lesson. On the first occasion they demanded water, which God told Moses to give them by 'commanding' a rock, staff in hand, to gush forth (Numbers 20:8). Moses and Aaron, by now more angry than ever, went beyond that. Moses struck the rock with his staff, having shouted at the people, 'Listen, you rebels, shall we bring water for you out of this rock?' (Numbers 20:10). Water came, but God was displeased that Moses had exceeded his brief and—more seriously—claimed for Aaron and himself the power to bring forth water. Their penalty (rather a harsh one, by human standards) was that neither of them would actually enter the promised land (Numbers 20:1–13).

After successful battles with several of the tribes, who were routed by the Israelites, and after the death of Aaron on Mount Hor, the people had one more attempt at mutiny. Annoyed by the devious route that Moses was taking, and again alleging that they were short of food and water, they spoke 'against God and against Moses' (Numbers 21:5). This time the penalty was for the camp to be overrun by poisonous snakes, whose venom was countered only by a brass image of a snake on a pole, which Moses carried through the camp. Those who looked at it were healed.

Through all such tribulations the long journey continued. God had promised that their coming to the promised land would be delayed by forty years, a year for every day that the spies had spent exploring Canaan (Numbers 14:34), so that no one then over twenty years old should enter the promised land. Eventually, of course, when the older generation had died, but still led by the venerable figure of Moses, the Israelites came to the plains of Moab on the borders of Canaan. The promised land lay ahead of them across the Jordan. Their long journey, marked with trials, tribulations, failings and triumphs, was at last nearing an end.

Moses, sensing that his own end was at hand, supervised the apportioning of the land they were to conquer and made his moving farewell speech (Deuteronomy 33). Then he climbed Mount Pisgah, from which he could at least view at a distance the land of promise. There he died, and was buried in the plains of Moab.

The Bible reading above takes us back, however, to the story of the spies and the rebellion sparked by their report. It captures both the faith of Moses and the fears of the people. Reading this, it seems strangely sad that both the courageous leader and the people he had led through good and ill on one of the greatest treks of human history were never to achieve their final goal. In their places would go two younger men, Caleb and Joshua, leading the next generation, most of whom would have been born on the journey and had no memory of the grim days in Egypt from which their parents had been so marvellously freed.

A reflection

Most of us can relate to the differing moods and reactions of the people on the journey. There can be few Christians who have not had moments when their faith has faltered—even, perhaps, when they have felt anger at God. I remember visiting a woman on the morning after she had found her husband dead in their home. As she opened the door, she launched herself at me, pummelling my chest and shouting, 'I hate God!' Weeks later she sought me out, shame-faced, to say how awful she felt about her reaction. 'I said that I hated God—will he ever forgive me?'

My answer was that God prefers honesty to pretence. The One whose Son took the blows on Good Friday out of love for the very people who were doing it could well take a few words uttered in the pain and distress of bereavement. The problem with the Israelites was not that they criticized God and his servant Moses, but that they disobeyed him because their faith was shallow.

On the long journey of life we all encounter setbacks, and there will inevitably be moments when doubts arise and faith falters. It is at those moments that the reality of our relationship with God is crucial. If we are truly his, even though at that moment we don't really 'feel' as though we are, then the words of our opening quote from the Bible are as valid for us as they were for the people of the old covenant: we too have a faith that remembers the faithfulness of God, a faithfulness that flourishes in the wilderness, 'where you saw how the Lord your God carried you, just as one carries a child, all the way that you travelled until you reached this place'.

EPITAPH FOR MOSES

DEUTERONOMY 34:1–12

Never since has there arisen a prophet in Israel like Moses, whom the Lord knew face to face. He was unequalled for all the signs and wonders that the Lord sent him to perform in the land of Egypt, against Pharaoh and all his servants and his entire land, and for all the mighty deeds and all the terrifying displays of power that Moses performed in the sight of all Israel (vv. 10–11).

The story of Exodus is essentially the story of Moses, or perhaps we ought to say, God and Moses. Hope for the enslaved Israelites first springs from the birth of a baby boy to an anonymous Hebrew family in Goshen. It grows with the child's remarkable preservation and eventual upbringing at the royal court. It survives a temperamental outburst that leads to his flight to the desert of Midian: indeed, rather more, God uses the event to bring the potential leader of the people to a unique encounter with him at the burning bush. In all of this, the reader is aware of a providential purpose. The story always seems to be going somewhere. There is a sense of divine purpose in the narrative.

The turning point in the life of Moses occurred in the Sinai region, standing in front of the burning bush. Here he was confronted by the purpose of God, spelt out to him with a clarity he could not deny. Despite all his protestations, he found himself called and commissioned to be the one who would confront the mighty Pharaoh and eventually lead the people to freedom. He may have seemed a reluctant hero, but once called it is fair to say that he never wavered in his determination to do what God required.

In all of this, Moses is typical of the biblical model of the 'man of God'. There is no attempt to depict him as a swashbuckling hero. The record is frank about his doubts, confusions and human frailties. In the end, this outstanding leader of his people was to be denied the satisfaction of entering the promised land to which he had so tenaciously led them, because, under great emotional strain, he had momentarily lost control and tried to take a particular issue into his own hands instead of leaving it to God.

So there is honesty in the picture the Bible presents us of this great leader, as there is in its portrayal of other great heroes— Samson, David, Solomon, Elijah and many others. Moses was a great man. It is clear about that. But he was a man marked by human frailties as well as strengths. And the clue to his greatness is given here in one sentence: 'He was unequalled for all the signs and wonders that the Lord sent him to perform… and for all the mighty deeds and terrifying displays of power that Moses performed in the sight of all Israel'. 'The Lord sent him to perform… Moses performed'—you simply can't see the join! He was God's instrument, without ceasing to be the personality that made him what he was.

There is the secret of Christian service, indeed of all Christian vocation. God uses human beings to fulfil his purposes, but does it without depriving them of their humanity. Many a man or woman called to a particular ministry or service is anxious, certainly at first, about the thought of a commitment so total that they cease to be themselves. The story of Moses tells us that we need not worry. Although his relationship with God was so close that the writer can say that the 'Lord knew him face to face' (v. 10), it was never so excluding that he ceased to be Moses—any more than Peter the apostle ceased to be the impulsive, passionate man who had fished the lake of Galilee, or Thomas the sceptical, down-to-earth pragmatist who wanted to see the evidence.

'Never since has there arisen a prophet in Israel like Moses' (v. 10). That is some epitaph! His greatness lay in his deeds, of course—a massive achievement, a model of leadership, courage and faith. It also lay in that spirit of co-operation with God which seems to be the hallmark of spiritual greatness. 'The Lord performed; Moses performed.'

His death in the land of Moab is recorded, after he had been shown from the hilltop the very land for which he had dedicated a great part of his life. 'I have let you see it with your eyes', said the Lord, 'but you shall not cross over there' (v. 4). It is interesting to see the chronicler's emphasis on Moses' physical well-being right to the end, 'sight unimpaired and… vigour not abated' (v. 7). It reminds us of the 'men of old', like Methuselah, in the early chapters of Genesis, who were said to have lived to be hundreds of years old. At least it reminds us that it is not a sin to be old! Indeed, until modern times, age (and the older the better) was taken to be a sign of great wisdom and great blessing from God.

The crucial factor in Moses' life, and the 'secret of his success', was clearly in his relationship with God, this 'face to face' knowledge. It doesn't say that Moses knew God face to face—indeed, we are told that although he pleaded to see the divine features, the sight was denied him. The blessing was the other way round—not his knowledge of God, but God's knowledge of him. It was that knowledge which enabled God to entrust Moses with mighty deeds, trusting him, as the letter to the Hebrews says, 'as a faithful servant in God's house'. There was one who was not only perfectly known by God, but also perfectly knew his will, and in the same passage the comparison is made: 'Jesus is worthy of more glory than Moses… Christ was faithful over God's house as a son' (Hebrews 3:2–6).

Moses, in other words, was not divine, but that is simply stating the obvious. He was a man. But among men he was a giant, and his greatness derived from his closeness to his Creator. Perhaps that is the secret of all true greatness?

A reflection

To be called by God is not to be 'taken over' but to be made a co-operator with his purposes. It is one of the miracles of grace that even the most unpromising material, humanly speaking, can be taken by him and transformed, but never annihilated. As the worship song says, 'Jesus, take me as I am, I can come no other way'.

OVER JORDAN

JOSHUA 3:1–17

While all Israel were crossing over on dry ground, the priests who bore the ark of the covenant of the Lord stood on dry ground in the middle of the Jordan, until the entire nation finished crossing over the Jordan (v. 17).

'My home is over Jordan' sang the slaves in the cotton plantations 200 years ago. They certainly needed a 'homeland', being far away from the Africa of their birth, but the one they looked for was the heavenly one that God would one day take them to, when all the labour and humiliation and rough treatment were over. There, God would wipe every tear from their eyes. There would be no more 'mourning and crying and pain' (Revelation 21:4). It was a rich vision, captured for all time in the words of their spiritual songs. From them, the idea of death as 'crossing Jordan', entering a new and wonderful land 'flowing with milk and honey', became part of the poetry of faith.

But first Jordan had to be crossed. Historically speaking, it's hard to locate exactly where the Israelites were to cross it, but all along its length it is hardly of Amazonian proportions. Still, any river was a barrier to a people who were herding cattle and dragging wagons with them, not to speak of small children and the elderly. They also now had the cart bearing the 'tent of meeting', the tabernacle of God's presence, which was handled with supreme reverence. They were not going to risk losing that to the current, rocks or pot-holes that provided the normal hazards of a river crossing.

The promised land lay beyond. At last, after 40 years of seemingly endless desert wanderings, they were on the verge of their heritage. God had promised them a rich, fertile land, with fruit and water in abundance. Those who had made it to this point were mostly young, the original travellers having fallen under the judgment of God for their faithlessness. Few of them could even remember the Egypt their parents had left, and for those who could, they would have been childhood memories. But they all knew the story. They knew the power and the promises of God. They had followed Moses, the man with whom God had talked 'face to face', as to a 'friend'.

Here, in the plain of Moab, as they waited and planned (and once again sent out spies ahead), Joshua, the anointed successor of Moses, assumed the role both of military leader and of the bearer of God's words to the people. Like Moses when they left Egypt, Joshua faced trial by water. Their journey had begun with the crossing of the Reed Sea, made possible solely by the power of the Lord. That crossing led to a long and wearisome journey. Now it was to reach its fulfilment with the crossing of another stretch of water, the River Jordan, but this time the crossing would lead to a 'place of rest' (Joshua 1:13).

It's not surprising that down the ages people have read these stories as parables of the life of faith. The apostle Paul draws the parallel between the crossing of the Reed Sea by Moses and the Israelites and Christian baptism (1 Corinthians 10:2). Both mark the start of a long, and at times necessarily wearisome, journey. Both eventually lead to the Jordan, and across it is the 'land of rest'.

The detailed instructions for the crossing mirror in many ways the crossing of the Reed Sea. Joshua is cast in the role of a second Moses. It is he who commands the column and bears the instructions of God to the priests and people. This time there is no pillar of cloud to lead them, but there is something even more significant, the ark of the covenant. The people are told to follow it, as it was borne on the shoulders of the Levitical priests, 'so that you may know the way you should go, for you have not passed this way before' (v. 4). Again, the people are told to 'sanctify themselves'. This is not a human enterprise, but a divine one. They will cross the river and enter the land entirely at the Lord's bidding and by his strength. And—a final touch—once they were safely over, the people were to celebrate Passover, the very ritual that had originally brought their release from Egypt.

Clearly the writer is trying to tell us something! This event, the crossing of the Jordan, is the completion of the task God had promised to fulfil. He had said that he would bring them to a 'good land, flowing with milk and honey', and he had. It had taken forty years, but most of those years were spent learning the painful lessons of disobedience. God led them out of Egypt, God led them across the waters of the Reed Sea, God fed them in the wilderness, God gave them his laws and made them his covenant people; and now, in a final act of wonder, he brings them into the land of promise.

The crossing is beautifully described. The priests carried the ark towards the river at Joshua's command. The people followed at a reverent distance—2,000 cubits, about 800 metres. As the feet of the priests touched the waters, the river dried up, although at that time of the year the spring floods would have ensured an overflowing current. The waters of the Jordan, we are told, were blocked off far away to the north, with no water at all flowing on towards the Dead Sea to the south. The priests with the ark stood still in the middle of the river bed and the people streamed across, led by armed men from three of the tribes.

Joshua had chosen twelve men, one from each tribe, for a special ceremonial task. They were to gather twelve stones from the very place where the priests had stood and carry them to the other side. The stones were erected in Gilgal as a permanent reminder of the day when God brought the twelve tribes across the Jordan into the promised land. Just as children at the Passover would ask, 'What does this mean?' so, it says, in the future children would ask what those stones meant. They were to be told the story of the crossing of the Jordan on the day when the Lord cut off the waters of the river to allow the ark of the covenant and the covenant people to cross on dry ground.

Here was a true 'epiphany' indeed, a 'showing forth' of the glory of God. After many trials and tribulations, his people had been vindicated. The surrounding tribes, the ancient world, history itself, could bear witness. What he had said he would do, the Lord had done.

Across the Jordan the people were to find their promised inheritance. For them there were battles yet to come, for although the land had been given to them by the Lord, they had yet to 'possess' it. But this was the great moment of transition. The feet that had been worn sore by the burning sand and the rock-strewn trail now stood on Canaan's land. Moses had looked at the promised land from the mountain-top, but had not entered it with them. It is hard to doubt, however, that the heart of the faithful leader was with them as at last 'they entered into their rest'.

A reflection

It's easy to see what led the hymn writer Isaac Watts to draw from this story a parable of the Christian facing death. 'There is a land of pure delight', he wrote:

> **Sweet fields beyond the swelling flood**
> **stand dressed in living green;**
> **so to the Jews old Canaan stood**
> **while Jordan rolled between.**

But the mortal heart holds back. The river is deep and wide. The prospect beyond seems frightening:

> **Timorous mortals start and shrink**
> **to cross the narrow stream.**

The promise may be inviting, but the process of attaining it seems perilous and dreadful. Watts turns to the picture of Moses on Pisgah:

> Could we but climb where Moses stood
> and view the landscape o'er,
> not Jordan's stream, nor death's cold flood,
> should fright us from the shore.

Doubtless that is true, but even for the man or woman of faith, to whom death itself is a gateway to eternal life, the actual process of dying is a daunting prospect. Will 'Jordan' really divide to let us over? Will the 'ark of the covenant' truly stand in its midst as the promise of the presence of God? Because death is something that always, by definition, happens to someone else, few of us can know how we will find the event.

Yet, as someone who has recently shared (if that's the right word) in the dying of someone very special and precious to me, the one thing I have learnt is the certainty of the presence of God. 'When you walk through the valley of the dark shadow, I am with you' (Psalm 23:4). That is not a promise that there will never be a 'valley of dark shadow', but only that God will walk with us through it, as he walked with the Israelites across Jordan into the promised land. Only! What an inadequate word!

The 'wilderness trail' of the life of faith will inevitably take us through dark places (though there will be moments of feasting and joy as well), but with angelic hands and signs and wonders of his love God has promised never to leave us or forsake us. Despite all their failure and disobedience, God stayed with his people of old in the wilderness. 'I am with you,' said Jesus to the disciples of the new covenant, 'even to the end of the age.' That is the promise that should see us safely 'over Jordan'.

GROUP DISCUSSION
MATERIAL

Cruel bondage (1–5 December)

1. How can the group relate to the description of the Hebrews' plight in Egypt? What kinds of 'bondage' do we experience—to a task, to a relationship, to an employer, to stifling circumstances? And how do we think of the idea of being 'slaves to sin' (Romans 6:20)? Hardly a popular idea in modern thought—but what truth is there in the concept of 'sin' (however we define it) shackling our lives?

2. The Hebrews seemed incapable of making a united response to their slavery. Some, like the midwives, dealt with it in their own circumstances as best they could; others seem to have fallen into a numb despair. In what way do members of the group sympathize with these responses from their own experiences?

3. It seems that fervent prayer was long delayed—or perhaps the Hebrews had simply despaired of ever being heard? God was acting towards their freedom even before they asked! So—how important is the asking? Thinking of the story of the birth of Moses, what do you feel this tells us about God's 'providence'— or was it just 'coincidence'?

The burning bush (6–10 December)

1. Do you think Moses had settled for life as an 'alien', with a new wife and family in a new land? If so, where was his faith in the

God of his fathers? How easy is it for us simply to 'accept' a situation, even when we wish things were different? Have any members of the group got personal experience of that?

2. What does the group make of the encounter at the burning bush? How do you envisage the scene, and the 'conversation'? Why do you think God's 'name' and identity matter so much to Moses? Thinking about the title 'I AM', what (if anything) does it say to the group about the nature of God? What does it mean to believe that God is 'eternal', without beginning or ending?

3. Moses' excuses—does anyone in the group relate to them from personal experience? ('You can't mean me, God!'). As the excuses are raised, so they are met. Is that our experience of God's call, or not?

The plagues and the Passover (11–16 December)

1. What do you think is the essential difference between magic and miracle? Do these stories throw any light on it? What was the miraculous element in the plagues, most of which were not uncommon phenomena in those days? And in what way was the final plague different from the others?

2. Pharaoh and his hardened heart—is there a problem here for people in the group? How would you distinguish between Pharaoh hardening his heart, God hardening Pharaoh's heart, or the heart of Pharaoh 'being hardened'? Is personal responsibility for action preserved in the biblical story, or compromised? In what ways, then, was Pharaoh guilty?

3. Discuss the Passover—have any members taken part in a Passover *seder*? How did it strike them? Was it principally an exercise of faith or obedience? And what would be the effect on the

Hebrew people of celebrating this feast year by year? (If possible, it might be interesting to get hold of a copy of the Passover liturgy and read it through together.)

Rescued, guided, provided (17–22 December)

1. Crossing the Red (or Reed) Sea was to be seen throughout their future as the great moment of emergence for Israel. What was God's role in their escape, and what was theirs?

2. Do members of the group find the imagery of the pillars of fire and cloud helpful as pictures of God's guidance and protection? Have any of them personal experiences of being 'led' or protected by God in different moments of need?

3. 'Give us this day our daily bread'—do you connect this prayer with the idea of the heavenly manna, given day by day? Having brought his people into a wilderness, do you feel that God was under an obligation to provide food for the journey? And what, if anything, does this say to the Christian pilgrim today? Jesus spoke of the manna and his own body and blood in the same discourse (John 6:32, 47–56). In what ways might Christians see the Eucharist as a similar 'food for the journey'?

The final battles (23 December–6 January)

1. What does it mean to the group to 'put the Lord to the test'? What's the difference between that and asking God for a sign? (See Luke 4:12.) What was the basic sin in the constant 'murmurings' and 'complaining' of the people?

2. How does the group distinguish between the moral law (Ten Commandments) and the ritual and civil law which was also

given to Israel? How would you answer this question: 'Do you think the Ten Commandments (all of them) apply today?' Do you find that Jesus' summary of the law helps you to understand and apply them? (Mark 12:30–31).

3. Taking the story of the crossing of Jordan, in what ways do group members find it helpful in relation to the end of the Christian pilgrimage to the promised land? Has anyone an experience to share about the death of a Christian which might illuminate the idea of the presence of God in the middle of the dark waters?

For further reading

Godfrey Ashby, *Go Out and Meet God*, Eerdmans/Handsel Press, 1998.

G. Henton Davies, *Exodus*, Torch Bible Commentaries, SCM Press, 1967.

Alan Cole, *Exodus*, IVP, 1973.

Frances Hogan, *Words of Life from Exodus*, Fount, 1984.